Thank you, Mrs. Canvas,
for giving me a ton of second chances, for your
incessant encouragement and your
unbreakable love.

Thank you, Canvas Jr.,
for always making my day
with your love and laughter.

Thank you, Daily Prompt, for re-igniting my
passion to create, and for creating a place for
expression and growth.

Thank you, Prompt-folk,
for never telling me I couldn't do it and for
tolerating my ramblings! You all are so
incredibly inspiring.

Thank you, reader, for your support!

DIVI

SION

That 'why', hanging in my chest like a blade,

to answer would be to rip it out.

And honestly....

I'm not sure.

I'm certain you know what I'm going on about.

I know you'll read this quietly,
but it'll be so loud.

And I hope your heart,
silently beings to pound.

I long for that sound.

It'll be painfully obvious,
but it won't change a thing.

I guess that division runs far,
far deeper than we ever thought it would.

I'll pull the blade out on three...

You ready for a flood?

One of emotions I've bottled, of hate and of blood?

It's long overdue,

but the time has finally come...

Just like I always knew it would.

You asked for this, Canvas.

You sat still, when you should've stood.

'Why'

I'm sure that boy is here somewhere.

He must be. I can't be empty.

He must be scattered upon
the vast plains of
repressed memories.

He grew twice as quickly,
producing a giant man
with half the heart.

I look for him often,
maybe that's why I'm immature.

That's probably why I'm immured in your curvatures,
a carnivorous carrier of the child's character caricature.

That little lad
shaking a fist at the sky,
asking the Son
for an explanation,
longing to know
why he had to die.

That boy limped
through life with
his soul severed,
but I know he's still here.

We're tethered together.

Those days spent planning
split decisions,
little incisions
to make everything
else feel numb…
a twisted rule of thumb.

They left him alone,
so far from a broken home.
He refused to drop crumbs,
too wise to follow 'em
back to bums.

If I ever do find him,
I just want to know
what he'd think of me,
you see?

I was the only one
in his corner for so many years…

I think I need to find him…
so that I can finally shed his tears.

I wish I could take his fears,
those terrors that left me here,

                    searching for a boy…

so far away…

                            …and impossibly near.

'Scrying'

She sleeps in my palms,
beneath crossed fingers,
praying through Psalms,
but my grip yet lingers.

Oh, she weeps,
under my eyes,
urging me to cry.

She filters the secrets I keep.
She separates the half-truths
from white lies, scouring me for love.

She's my little trophy,
her heart so full of atrophy
in light of my atrocity.
I cannot help her agony.

It's always just her and me.

She sleeps in my palms,
beneath my rotting thumbs,
whispering her hymns,
into my hollow limbs.

Her soft eyes are open wide,
she stares weakly into mine,
upon my lying, splitting tongue,
this little broken trophy is hung.

She prays I will change.
She begs for the day.
She will hide the pain.
She won't leave but she can't stay.

She can't stay here in my palms.

She pleads to a heart of stone,
that it might break
when morning comes.

Sleep, my love, upon my dreams.

My trophy of what I gave up,

what is this nightmare I've become?

Rest your head and make me new.

What is this I have done to you?

She sleeps in my palms,
though my hands are numbed.
She dreams of my end,
where we can start again.

She sleeps now and dreams of me.

I can't sleep for agony.

My dreams are all atrophied,

trophies for my casualties.

Rest in peace, my love...

'Upon My Palms'

That apprehension,
my chest,
tight with tension.

Standing at the edge of your eyes,
staring into my reflection.

Climbing, clumsily up your lashes,
dangling over the ocean as the waves reach up for me.

Of course, I'm terrified to jump into your eyes.

I'm horrified that you might find the nothingness in mine.

And so, slowly, I watch your eyes turn black.

Now I have to jump in,
but it's worse now...
because I waited to show
you what you're worth.

I've made that ocean,
once calm and gentle,
into a storm of blood and tears,
swirling together
over the course of years.

I just need to swallow my fears

and fall into your eyes.

If I wait any longer…

I know you
won't see me at all.

'Into Your Eyes'

Another midnight bloom,
breathing unlit fumes.

They're begging for ignition, gently humming a mute tune to the deafened moon.

My circadian rhythm,
the petals rehearse each night - as their cicada wings circumvent my rapid eyes.

A cataclysmic chorus of husks just waiting to happen, they'll see their days waste away, just like mine,

sowing seeds, laying eggs, inside my brain, praying they'll thrive, and I'll break.

Swaying to and fro, thorns like bittersweet dreams plague my mind.

How I adore the one that clings to my side like a knife.

Nightshade consumes me like the moonless sky swallows light.

Like sweet dreams,
those petaling wings,
like a thousand guttural screams,
mesmerizing every seam inside me.

Stitching everything I've seen to the things I desired.

Those lovely petals, they long for fire.

And I swear,
I'm so tired,

I may light a match.

'Nightshade'

I just keep laughing it off.

I know that if I stop...

everything will catch up to me,

so I have to pretend it's all still funny.

I can laugh to anything.

Everything horrifying is humorous.

I can't take serious things seriously.

I just laugh it off as if they're amusing to me.

I know that makes me empty.

Empty, but full of apathy.

I wonder if it's because they laughed at me...

Hell, I guess I finally get the joke at least.

Maybe one day these little chuckles will turn to tears...

Like they're supposed to be.

I guess I'll see.

Maybe it's all a joke anyway,

and I'm just a punchline gone astray.

Or am I in the front row, watching it all go over my head?

I'm just going to do my best not to laugh today.

'Punchline'

Your golden boy has grown.
You weren't there to see it.
Your golden boy has grown,
a xanthous horror in a pit.

Oh, the man I've become!

Oh, what gold!

Oh, the blood!

Oh, that you'd reach
your hands out to me!

Only cruel pyrite you'd cling.

I cannot save you.

You cannot blame me.

You have raised me to kill.
You have raised me for thrills.
You gave me life to die.
What a luminous lie!

Your golden boy,
has lost his shine.

Mother,
this man of gold,
is pyrite.

'Pyrite'

They said the first year would be the hardest.

How absolutely thoughtless!

That first year was a blast, we we're moving just as fast...

I wish that first year had never passed.

I wish that first year replaced the last.

I think we used to smile a lot.

It's been so long... I think I forgot.

Was it year three or four when things started to fall apart?

I guess that says a lot...

I can't remember the first time I broke your heart...

Does that make it more or less beautiful...
 that year fourteen is about to start?

I think light feels so much warmer...

when it's surrounded by dark.

That doesn't mean I wouldn't go back to that first year.

I'd go back and make sure that you didn't ever have a reason
to shed a single tear.

I'd make sure you had nothing to fear, my dear.

But, we're here in this year.

Let's just hold these moments near.

'First Year'

When I awake,
    I'm sound asleep.

I start each day,
    living a dream.

I say to you,
    the things I think.

You say to me,
    'It's just dreamspeak.'

                  Maybe I'm delirious,
            maybe there's a point I missed.

Maybe this is lucid dreaming,
I can't tell cause my hearts beating.

            Pinch me please,
                and end my sleeping.

            Kill me please,
                and end my pleading.

If this is life,
        then what's the meaning?

If this is love,
        then what's the screaming?

Wake me up,
and end this being.

I'm wide asleep,
and so I dreamspeak.

You're sound awake,

                but you're not listening.

                  'Dreamspeak'

You are always so caring.
You'd cry an ocean if the world caught fire,
inadvertently saving the day.

I love that about you, by the way.

I wish I could have that care...

If the world caught fire, I'd probably be the arson, scolding
himself for forgetting to bring marshmallows, you know?

It just makes it funny that we're so close.

We always said we couldn't wait to grow old.

Here I am freaking out that I'm going grey just before thirty.

But when I saw one silver hair on your head....
my heart started hurting.

I think I put it there,

with all the years of pain and worry.

I really wish I could have that care.

I bet that little silver hair wouldn't be there.

On the bright side,

   you look wonderful in grey.

You look wonderful in everything.

                    Do you smell something...

                              'Burning?'

Like a mimic,
breaking once more upon my mind -

a harmony now embedded.

The sound greets my
eyes as a corpse's kiss,
reverberating sleepless
nights and mourning's bliss.

Compose me.

                    Plagiarize.

Compose me.

                    Harmonize.

Compose me.
          Resonate blades sent by light's last cry.

Whisper unto me,
those naked secrets.

Scream in my face,
the only taste I crave.

Lying next to me,
I wallow in dishonesty.

That decade, a hum,
a cataclysmic ohm.

Compose me.
I won't be without your touch.

Compose me.
Fill my life with your color.

Compose me.
Tear me apart,

I just want your heart.   *'Mimicry'*

A severed man,
connected by a ghost
that he hid inside.

Separated from the rest,
he will watch them die.

His arms are his legs,
and his legs are his hands.
His hands hold his eyes,
on his pupils he'll stand.

He sees them walk,
over him on right feet.
He sees them walk,
but he can't bend his knees.

The man tries to talk,
but the people, they leave.

The man tries to live,
but his life starts to flee.

The mouth on his chest,
spreads its lips gleefully.

This man tilts his head,
starts to laugh,

 and then screams.

'Not Quite Natural'

I see myself in mirrors,

embedded in my skin.

I see myself in mirrors,

as me looks back at him.

I cannot stare too long,

else I'll be trapped within,

the thousand little mirrors,

reflecting bygone sins.

I cannot linger there,

or I'll be him again.

I see myself in mirrors,

reflecting from within.

All too often,

 I wish...

   to never see again.

All too often,

I think...

   these mirrors will be my end.

'Mirrorskin'

So, I dreamed up a spider,
and I watched it leave my head.

It claimed that it was starving,
and soon it would be dead.

The spider started spinning,
a rather handsome web.

Before I even knew it,
that nice web was my new bed.

Within that fibrous prison,
I hadn't any fear.

The spider seemed disgruntled,
that I hadn't shed a tear.

The demon sunk its fangs,
deep into my bleeding heart...

A heart that wasn't beating,
and was never going to start.

The spider was befuddled,
by my lack of tasty blood.

I looked to her and smiled,

"Look, I've only words and mud."

'Disappointment'

I'm
sinking
under
the
burden, As I swallow my spit,
                    now my
grinning,   brittled
I'll bear it.   teeth   The dirt swallows my feet,
                    split.   my bones are splintering.

The judges crash their
        glass hands to one another,
                        a shrapnel shower.   Surely the laughs
                                                                of the last
                                                                of the hours.

                            Lifting it all,
I give all to stand tall.
                        The last thing I'll do
before I take my fall.

                A final applause for a final audition!

Screaming my lungs
out with internal attrition!
I outweigh these convictions,
and to hell I'm conditioned!

And the lines I've forgotten,
                                line my arms, line my skin!

They just speak for themselves,
                                and the judges, they love it.

They stand and they shout,
                                but the sounds won't come out.

Oh, I think I may cry,
                        but they've put out my eyes.

Now, I think I may die,
                    but my life is not mine.

What sort of man would I be,
                        If I didn't play the part?

Now they cast someone else,
                            a mere shade of myself!

So I rip out my heart,
                    hold it up,   call it art.

On this canvas, a stage,
I will pour out my rage.
I will tear down myself,
Judges please look away!

Now the pages lie barren!
        Now the world is in flames!
                    Now I recall the lines,

I say,
        "We're all the same!"

And the weight crushes me!
And behold!
                        I'm empty.

And the judges all scream,
And behold!
                    They can't see!

Now the crimson seas fall,
they just wash over me!

                    I awake from the dream.

            And behold!

    I'm not me.   *'They Want a Show'*

Another madman,
hastily scribbling dribble,
nonsensical verses for the scholars to mock.

Those starving scholars,
like lunatics laughing at a timeless clock,
 folding their fingers over the hour hand,
 begging it to stop.

The Wiseman's hearty laugh flows wrongly to the mouth of
folly, exhaling the rot.

We have here this Curvecoat,
giving himself a hug because no one else did.

 Self-care was a pit they pushed him in, on a whim.

Maybe I'll dive in and take a swim.

I'll sink into the sky, assuming I can fly, as THE END passes
me by, stopping to question me why I never asked for wings.

It'll go, on and on, about all the hope it brings... singing such
things in far higher octaves than my final screams...

And I'll land in the clouds, right where you came from.

Deep down, in those clouds...

I'll realize that I always belonged in the ground.

What if the divide is really just a lie?

What if we spent all this time,
cutting ourselves with fine lines?

Well, that's my time.

Today is the day.

I'm...   *'On My Way'*

Dad is in the kitchen,
making needle tea.
Mom is in a hurry,
the methadone is calling.

The leaking fridge is empty,
your stomach eats itself.
Your little brother hits the pipe,
and it's filled with only hell.

You are a flower,
growing in a landfill.
Dad always wanted to fight you,
but he'd only run from me.

You are a flower,
growing in the flames.
In all of my days,
I've not seen such strength.

You lay your head on a pillow,
one of trash and mold.
This home is not home.
It's an abandoned house.

They did not shape you.
And you could not save them.
You are the strongest
person that I know.

You are so much
stronger than me.
You are a flower,
that spends its days with me.

And I am a fool,
with nary a sense of smell.
You are the strongest
person that I know.

You are a flower,
the most beautiful flower.
You are a flower...

...how could you forgive me?

'For When You Feel Weak'

XXXXXXX~~WE~~XXXXXXXXXXXXXXXXXXXXXXXXXX
XXXXXXXX~~LOOK~~XXXXXXXXXXXXXXXXXXXXXXXX
XXX~~FOR~~XXXXXXXXXXXXXXXXXXXXXXXXXXXXXX
XXXXXXXXXXXXXXXX~~WHAT~~XXXXXXXXXXXXXX
XXXXX~~WE~~XXXXXXXXXXXXXXXXXXXXXXXXXXXX
XXXXXXXXXXXXXXXXXX~~ARE~~XXXXXXXXXXX
XX~~INSIDE~~XXXXXXXXXXXXXXXXXXXXXXXXXXX
XXXXXXXXXXXX~~OF~~XXXXXXXXXXXXXXXXXXXX
XXXXXXXXXXXXXXXXXXXXXXXXXXXX~~A~~XXXXX
XXX~~BOX~~XXXXXXXXXXXXXXXXXXXXXXXXXXXX
XXXXXXXX~~PRETENDING~~XXXXXXXXXXXXXX
XXX~~THAT~~XXXXXXXXXXXXXXXXXXXXXXXXXXX
XXXXXXXXXXXXXXXXXX~~WE~~XXXXXXXXXXXXX
XXX~~ARE~~XXXXXXXXXXXXXXXXXXXXXXXXXXXX
XXXXXXXXXXXXXXXXXX~~NOT~~XXXXXXXXXXX
XXXXX~~IN~~XXXXXXXXXXXXXXXXXXXXXXXXXXX
XXXXXXXXXXXXXXXXXXXXXXX~~IT~~XXXXXXXX
XXX~~OPEN~~XXXXXXXXXXXXXXXXXXXXXXXXXX
XXXXXXXXXXXXXXXXXXXXXXXXXX~~THE~~XXX
XXXXXXXX~~BOX~~XXXXXXXXXXXXXXXXXXXXX

And	I	When	I	Are	I
Where	I	We	I	The	I
Will	I	Finally	I	Box	I
We	I	Discover	I	?	I
Look	I	That	I	To	I
Next	I	We	I	Division	I

~~as we always do.~~

'The Box'

Faces buried into phones,
burrowed into one another.

Hundreds of them, soaked in
yellow lights lining the streets.

Seeped in echoes of each other
- the embrace of brothers,
of friends, and lovers.
                    And I am alone.
               And I wonder…
                         if they are alone too.

I think they're alone, with everyone.

I wonder if they see me, a vagrant.
I felt invisible back then.

Now, I feel invisible still,
as I blend in with the night.
With everyone,   I am alone.

And I wonder if their joy is a façade,
as I hear their laughter as they hold each other close.

And I wonder if they've ever lost.
        I wonder if their lives,   they loathe.

The city is poised to claim my soul,
and so, I wonder…

                 will anyone know?

And so, I walk,
alone with them.
Everyone is here,
but I've got no friend.

If they could see
        beneath my skin,
            would everyone
                    be alone again?   *'Alone Together'*

I wish you could cure me,
the way you long to.
To cure me of the disease,
yet it only spreads to you.

Give me a kiss.

I wish you could fix me.
Shape me into what you need.
I doubt I'd be what you expected,
you'd find yourself now twice infected.

Give me a kiss.

I think you'll have to break me.
The me that broke you.
Hold me close as I crumble.
Like bits of sand, slipping through you.

Give me a kiss.

I've got all the parts, but I lack the heart.

That's something you can't give.

Give me a kiss.

So, I will spread to yours, a malady to your pulse.

Give me a kiss.

And I'll hate you for becoming like me.

Give me a kiss.

If I could go back to that first kiss, I'd fix all this,
so that you wouldn't feel like you need to.

I'd never have to ask you to...

'Give Me a Kiss'

Beautiful eyes, staring at me.

Lost, as the love we had.

Oracles now barren, empty.

Only ashes remain,

Diluting the blood,

Leaving us hungering.

Eat, my love.

This heart is yours.

Taste of cruelty on thy tongue.

In the morning we die,

Never let go of tonight.

God, I wish this wasn't goodbye.

'Bloodletting'

Hate was a blessing,
        a place for the cursed.

 Love was a line,
        I had never rehearsed.

Fear was my prose and death every verse.

And I spoke in decay,
                'for better or worse.'

I know I heard you whisper that this was the end.

How can I keep I keep fighting if we'll never mend?

Why should we keep trying if we'll never win?

Are we just gonna make believe or play pretend?

You say we should call it quits and just be friends.

You sleep in the grass, and I'll stay on the fence.

You can't stand my absolute indifference.

When you start to cry, I have no tolerance.

Then I look to your eyes and fall in love again.

Just an hour later and we're laughs and grins.

I think you're an angel, but I feel I'm Grim.

I will watch you rise, and I know I'll descend.

I've said so many things I wish I could rescind.

I could write this piece all day,

        but this one needs to end.   *'Arguments'*

I smiled with a heart full of fear,
I laughed with a handful of hair.

They said it was too late.
They said they could try.
They gave me three months to live.
They gave me three months to die.

Three years later
and I'm still standing.
Those three months
didn't leave me stranded.
They only left me
stronger than I'd ever been.

So I wave goodbye.
With a head full of hair,
and a heart full of life.

Goodbye,
cancer.

I won't miss you.

And I damn sure won't
live under your shadow.

to the survivors, to the slain, to a buddy   *'Cancer'*

I painted her
with oil and coal,
on a canvas blank,
I worked and toiled.
Her beauty
I couldn't replicate,
she said 'I do',
it must be fate.

I painted her
with my affection.
For years I gave
her my attention.
I traced her
every single day,
those lines I drew
would never fade.

I painted her
with my mistakes.
My sin and shame,
on her engraved.
I've left her in
a shade of pain,
a canvas torn
from selfish ways.

Every stoke left her with another scar.
I painted that hell in her eyes.
The ink bled through to her heart.
I'll paint our way out of my lies.

Not by my hand alone…
Another will paint us a new life.
You know I can't erase.
Love, let's watch the canvas change.
I promised you all of my days,
no matter what,

 with you I'll remain.

'I Painted Her'

That kid,
 playing with sidewalk chalk,
 making little masterpieces.

That man,
outlined in chalk,
leaving strangers to pick up the pieces.

It's crazy what a difference twenty years is.

I remember that time I jumped off the trampoline, over a
huge bush, and no one was watching!

I remember standing on the edge, gently swaying, wiping
away tears, hoping that no one was watching.

      ...and begging someone to catch me.

It's crazy what a difference twenty years is.

I remember getting so sick as a boy, spending the night with
my head in a toilet.

I remember my teeth hurting from puking up those pills.

Maybe it's really not all that different.

Twenty years isn't that long anyway.

Maybe I'll go make another masterpiece on the sidewalk,

I think I'll just laugh if someone says something.

What if someone joined me?
That'd be quite the story.

Better than twenty stories, I think.

If you see a grown man playing with chalk,
that's me. If you want to join, feel free.

'Twenty Years'

Head down beneath the dirt,
this is your sanctuary.

Burrows carved through the slain,
your safety hinges
on a matter of inches.

The enemy nears the gates,
mindless heathens at the trenches.

Bullets of idle words and false gods kick up shrouds of
deception, painting the fields in rotting lies - the flies rush in
to devour.

The time has come to rise, one will obtain utter demise.

Elevate - this is the hour.

Speak your sermon of lead and gunpowder,
ripping conscious from
the ones without conscience.

Flashing lights fold over, one by one, through the sanguine
night.

If you aren't willing to die for it,
is it true?

You've said your peace -
life awaits as you
fall to pieces in the foxhole,
clutching your chest
and bleeding your soul.

You know what awaits you tomorrow.

You know they don't.

Because they enemy gets the divide.

'Foxhole'

We held hands as
we breathed our last.

We both just laughed
and laughed.

And I was there for you,
like I never was,
like I wish I would've been.

And the tears ran down
my face as I wore a grin.

They pulled the plug,
we came alive
- and we transcended.

You know I'd take
back what I said.

Those words I spoke
have left me dead.

And they killed you.

I'd do anything.

Anything to
make you feel.
Anything to
catch you when you fall.
I'd give it all
to let you heal.

When we go I know
we'll know that
this was never real.

When we die,
I know that love
will be revealed.

'Death'

I'll dim the lights.

For you, I'm sure they're twice as bright.

I wish I could see like you.

One day, they'll tell you that you aren't
                normal.

I'll make sure it stays quiet,
when you need some silence, my boy.

I wonder how you hear it,
if every sound is a symphony to amaze...
...or a raucous pitch to devastate.

I wish I could hear like you.

One day, they'll tell you that you aren't
                normal.

I'd never speak again
to hear you say something.

Anything.

You listen, absorbing it all with
your unique form of perception.

One day, they'll tell you that you aren't
                normal.

When they do,

 I need you to remember this...

'Your Normal is Exceptional'

You were so beautiful that day.

I know you weren't feeling well.

In sickness and in health, right?

I guess you got a head start
to a life of hell.

That black dress made your eyes shine.
As if they needed its help.
I was yours and you were mine,
I wish that ship never set sail.

I was wearing my fancy, new cement shoes.

If I recall correctly, that necktie was really just a rope noose.

I was dressed with all of my childhood issues.

I dove right in and hit the bottom,

and I took you too.

Where's that old ring again?

Lake Michigan?

Maybe I'll go for a swim.
    Maybe I'll give life and limb.
            I might do it on a whim!

Just to see you smile again.

(They):

:swore this was sink or swim.

(I):
:am sinking in my sin.

(You):

:cling to dreams of a man that has long since drowned.

A corpse.
Breathless, but breathing.
A clown.
With fancy, new cement shoes.

Why'd I have to take you with me?

I guess we've taken to a life of underwater breathing,
bleeding as we claw one another, desperately seeking a
surface that's fleeting. What's that feeling? It's the meaning,
suffocating in the dreaming.

I really never imagined
that I'd have led us here.

I really can't imagine
life without you, dear.

In sinking and in swimming,
you know I'll still be here.

I just really need to get some
new shoes,
you wait right there.

I really miss those peace shoes,
you got a pair?

'Fancy, New
Cement Shoes'

Please hold the makeup,
you know you don't need it.
The moment I wake up,
your beauty, I see it.

Bright green eyes
that glow in the light.
As I look into them,
I know it's alright.

Lips like honey,
a soothing balm,
one little kiss,
my pain is gone.

Skin so smooth,
Oh, those freckles too!

You haven't aged
a single day.
All these years,
your youth remains.

You know that when
we're old and grey,
I'll love you
like I do today.

You should know
your beauty
is much more
than your face.

Your true beauty is grace.

'The Visage of Beauty'

I keep watch over them.
A warden, eying his lot.
As in a world dreamt.

My prized possession.
A shame to have lost myself.
This crimson thing I've become.
Seeing through eyes that aren't mine.
As in a world dreamt.

Sight exposed dark lights -
disguised as allies.
Alluding to my demise.
Allured by the burning sky.
As in a world dreamt.

In a painted place.
A canvas of my design.
Torn by my lost mind.
As in a world dreamt.

Awakening me.
I am not myself.
Alas, I am no one else.
I will live today.
As in a world dreamt.

So I rise,
desperate to become,
anything but what I've done.

I will hold this pain,

As in a world dreamt.

'As in a World Dreamt'

His face,
contorted.
He refuses
to be comforted.

He flails to
the ground,
overwhelmed
by the sounds.

He rises. He bites. Drawing blood.
                    Queue the strange looks.
He screams.
The lights
are too bright.

He speaks his
discomfort -
through the look
in his eyes.
              They scoff,
              muttering what
                  they'd do.
Don't listen
to them, son.
Mom and Dad
are here for you.

    We hear you.
          We think it's too loud too.
                    Sorry they don't understand you.
If they were half as
bright as these lights,
they'd maybe even
stand with you.

You regulate the way
you feel you need to.

It doesn't change the fact
that Mom and Dad
both love you.   *'Stim'*

As I watched every reality,

collapse and unfold,

    my heart catching fire,

but my blood running cold...

I thought it wouldn't last.

Everything came to pass,

so, I put on that fractured mask...

I tried to take a deep breath,

but I only gasped...

       ... and so, I laughed:

In the face of time,

as it fell through my hands.

In the eyes of Death,

 as he breathed his last.

In the hands of life,

as I watched them die.

In the cursed light,

the dark made me blind.

There's a rule for me and you.

          You should know it's   '42'

Look at me.
What do you see?
You see a man,
a hollow thing?

Looking,
like a razor blade?
Cutting down the
wretched days?

Dancing in
a sea of rain,
I see you try
to hide the pain.

Look within
and search for truth.
They say the answers
deep inside you.

Scour you for
countless hours.
Find yourself,
you feel empowered?

Look around.
What do you see?
An extant dream
of misery?

I look and see,
you're just like me.

Look around,
things can be found.
Look real close,
you may see sound.

Search the skies,
and question why.

Look within,
and watch you die.

Look into
the eyes of night.
Blind yourself,
devoid of light.

Look at us!
We're such a sight!

Look into
my dying eyes.

Lean in close,
they're full of flies.

Kiss me,
taste my lying breath.

Look at me!
There's nothing left.

Watch me fade,
my soul take flight.

Look and see,
I saw a light.

'Look'

I want to be there
to catch that foul, sweet

wax, as it drips from your wings.
Lifting a glass for that wax,
I'll light a wick with my tongue

of fire - consuming your passions.
It's all I've ever wanted.
I'll propose a purposeless

toast to the wings that failed you.
My dear, you've failed them.
I'll raise a glass, pour out your

wrath so I can once again
writhe in the ash of your past.
It's all I ever wanted.
Please don't hesitate to

break for me. I'll raise
a glass to your eyes,
your tears, a remedy so
I might see - once and

for all. How great was the fall!

You're all I ever wanted.

'Raising a Glass'

Where will you fall?

What lies of black and white!

                    The truth is
                    in the middle.

A greyscale backdrop on monochrome programming,
another form of divide fed in small bytes, so

we will never fall for it. That honest fact,

that we aren't really all that different,

drowned in the static, stoically demanding that we're

nothing.

Alike, day and night, weave that hatred into the stars,

so that we can be guided to this side or

that. It's all dichotomy, a new definition given by society to

you and me. We aren't so different.

But we'll never be the same.

It'll never be enough to not choose a side,

but we've always been destined for

the divide.

            With your back to the wall...
                            'Where Will You Fall?'

I walk in and
see a beauty,

she orders tall
- but I say venti.

I swear she's sweeter
than this coffee.

I'm half and half cause…

she just kissed me.

Triple shot right
through my heart!

Cold brew stare -
a burning starts!

She licks her lips
of caramel foam,

and whispers,

"I'll see you at home."

'A Chance Encounter'

A boy, made of
mud and clay.

A child formed
by pain and hate.

A heart made stone
from years of pressure.

A man is asked
to stay together.

Crumbling from the
mud now dried,
the boy exposed,
the man can't cry.

A man of mud
and clay and pain,

the tears of a child,
now all in vain.

A new day brings
forth morning rain.

A man now washed,
is still unclean.

The boy inside,
now questioning,

what the hell
does it all mean?

The man of mud,
begins to scream.

Alike a pebble,
cursing the stone
it fell from.

Alike dirt,
destroying the
earth around it.

'Made of Mud'

Always told me
to be grounded.

I watched my life
flip upside down,

Stood up tall,
but made no sound.

I fixed my feet
on greyscale clouds,

I kept my head
up in the ground.

The dirt and worms
- I breathe - I drown.

My soles -
the skies just circle 'round.

You said I'd smile
- I wear a frown…

But you can't see
- I'm upside down.

'Head in the Grounds'

A gentle, verdant breeze,
spiraling, swirling with the tinge of an emerald

- whispering
upon my flesh.

Your eyes, a gale -

Calming.
Surreal.
Gentle.
A sea of leaves
waving
- as they see me.

Were it not me... I am wholly unworthy.

A storm of crystalline
pines - a tempest forms
as the rain pours from the fields.
A cyclone severing the meadows.
Emerging from them.

Your eyes, a gale.
Frightening roars of
agonized winds - hurling
everything I considered
static - peals of lightning
flashing among the
sage-colored clouds
- falling like rivers cutting
through the forest.

Your eyes,
a gale.

Your eyes,
a gale.

Your eyes,
have died.

'Your Eyes, A Gale'

In the darkness, we found it.

By the shadows, swear the heartless.

Like a raven's wings, carrying seeds to the thorns.

A maw full of maggots, whispering blasphemous utterances.

They can't understand because they aren't like us.

That blood defiled the negative space.

They see light and we see graves.

What was that one about the cardinals?

Do not speak of their countless martyrs.

It is profane.

We are better off divided.

They scourged us with their inquiries.

They preach from iniquity.

We are a disease?

We are.

So are they.

They are not our allies.

There must be

DIVI

In the light, we watch them die.

The sun illuminates tomorrow.

Those wings like eagles, shimmering like starlight.

Talons gripping glory, never to let go.

They can't understand because they aren't like us.

Blood shines through to extant grace.

They see dark, as they've no faith.

What of their horrors?

Say no more of their signs and wonders.

It is profane.

We are better of divided.

They drove us to near extinction.

Their sermons are hostility.

They say we've impurities?

We do!

They do too.

We cannot unite.

There must be

SION

Can't you taste
the water burning?

Bittersweet
memories of tomorrow,
a day that we lived already.

Flipping the page,
                outside in,
                        searching that
            cover for a meaning,
    from blank pages
pressed between what
                        we're gleaning…

nothing.

Stagnant and stoic,
a river washes over us.

Raging waters,
                burning,
Oh God,

listen to that hush.

Air leaving us breathless,
restlessness as we're
                sound asleep -
        listening to the
            songs of a mute siren.

Silence.

Roaring in our ears.

Painstakingly clothing ourselves in
agony,

     shrouding one another in

               sweet nothings

    - as the night sky stirs
       beneath our feet.

A cold heat - a slow burn
quickly consuming every second
we wasted in preparing for a dream.

Stitching a seam that the clouds left behind   - in front
of your eyes -   and right over mine.

You won't find him here.

That canvas is torn.

Hell, here's hoping!

He slammed the
door wide open.

Leave yourself behind,
and come on in.

All these words and nothing said,

that's just like you, old friend.

'Outside In'

Open skies beckon in
something broader.

Rolled away - like a scroll.
Revealing an expanse.
A wonder.
Taking my breath with it.

A never ending place - among the vastness of what we called
space.

Within the measure of
the things we called seconds.
Instants forming
into eternities.

To feel something -
indescribable -
written in what remains above me.

To see what was always there.
Hiding.
Behind a veil of stars
and singularities.

To quantify that longing.
That yearning for
something more.

To have substance
bestowed upon that
thing we called a soul.

And I stand here,
knowing to place
my face upon the floor.

To call it light,
To call it love,
To call it all,

would be silence.   *'As a Scroll'*

Hope only grows in the darkness.
It will only bloom in despair.

When the light withers
away - crumpled and
hollow under the
shadow's dismay,
Hope will spring from
the ashes of the corpse
they made.

It will not grow in the day.
It will not sprout within grace.

Hope demands pain.
It is nourished through blood.
It doesn't need rain.
It blossoms in fire and flood.

It is planted with the seeds of decay.
The world burns all around me.
I am everything I hate.
And hope grows in me.
The more I wish it'd die -
The more it clings to me.

Yet without it...

I wouldn't be here today.

'Hope'

An innocent question.
A small finger pointed.
The number is mentioned.
His heart is disjointed.

Her little finger,
tracing his arm
Her query still lingers,
a true answer meant harm.

"Six, four, two,
nine, eight."

Her sweet voice.

His heart ached.

"It means grandpa is tough.
You're tough too, aren't you Amelia?"

An excited nod.

"When do I get one too?"

"Grandpa will make sure
that you never will."

never forget   *'Grandpa's Tattoo'*

The
memories
of
longing
reached
for
her
under
a
cloudless
sky

- never
stopping
until
they'd
gently
tethered
her
shattered
mind,

       binding a blinded heart

- torn apart by a lustful lie.

To yearn :

- a tendril of hope
connecting two souls
- a tangled mess of love
- a burning passion

Unceasing.
Everlasting.

How can she be free?

To yearn...
it does bring misery.

'To Yearn'

Centuries of shadow,
eclipsing realities.

  We watch as reason bloomed from curiosity,
 but the meaning turned away.

All that to say, nothing.

Those skeptical ancients,
they pointed to tomorrow,
 crying sacrilege,
screaming grand words without sense.

All that knowledge lost,
a penalty for hastening doubt.

All that to say, nothing.

They're picking at their fangs with the bones of desecrated
youths, drinking from a fountain of me and you. What an isle
of inverted truth!

All that to say, nothing.

So, the crows decide what is forbidden,
souls in their wings hidden.
They won't fly for the lies will fall away and be written,

on another reject's wrists.

Sure, life is relentless.

Keep quiet.

They politely requested your silence.

              All that to say...

                      Shhhh......

                                  'Nothing'

Last night's dreams are tomorrow's nightmares.

They'll find their way back into today,
shredding your vision along the way.

Break.
It's okay.
Something they'd never say.

They didn't.

You only heard the catcher,
speaking endless tongues,
promising new beginnings
that will come at long last.

This too shall pass, words flowing like glass into your veins.

Choose your path from the forked speech inside.

There's always another half-truth to hide behind, another

complacent compilation of vain comprehensions to
press into your mind - so that the dreams stay inside the
pillow and you might live a day without them.

Run along. This piece is for a day that hasn't come, twin to
the one you relive all the day long.

Like a song in your head that you've never heard before.

Oh, all those lyrics you've come to adore!

It's the screaming you hear between three and four,
while you lay on the floor,

you can't take anymore.

But you won't accept...   *'Anything Less'*

You were there, with your My Chemical Romance shirt…
I miss that shirt, you know?

You had those fishnet sleeves, enrapturing - but those aren't
what captured me.

That little heart you'd painted on your cheek, it made me
weak in the knees,
but I didn't fall for it.

That long black hair, a beautiful snare, but I wasn't caught in it.

It was the way you didn't want to look at me. And the way I
didn't want to make it obvious. The way we caught eyes and
tried to pretend that the room didn't catch fire, like we were
oblivious.

It was your bright green eyes, you know, babe? I tripped right
into them.

I wish I'd have taken that first kiss, it hurt you that I didn't. But
I was a different kid back then and didn't want to spoil it.

You know you make me smile.
Without you I never would.
On the bad days, you're the only thing that can really bring
me down.

Sure, I don't have control over myself.

But as long as I have you, I don't need anything else.

This isn't an apology, just a memory,
of that day back in '09 - you got the best of me.

I wish you had the best of me now.

I really do.

'*Sure, I Don't
Have Control*'

A young Sprout,
at the edge of the
trees he planted.

He wanders about,
breathing the carbon
exhausted.

The trees breathe -
- the Sprout breathes.
The trees sway -
- the Sprout sees.

Each one lined just
as he'd instructed them.

Two branches above -
and two below,

as far as the Sprout can see.

Their features vary only slightly.

Each one filled with
the same sweet sap.

Sprout sits beneath
an ancient one -
his leaves rustling
against the tree's flesh.

Sprout sweetly laughs as the
tree's toes wiggle in the sky.

Sprout loves the trees.

He's not sure why.

'As a Tree'

Leaves gathered
about the branches.

Waving to one another.
Waving to The Tree.

Connected.
A family.
A sea of faces,
graced by the Son.

The cold breeze is nothing.
A chill down their spines.
A vapor - like the leaves.

I fall - calling for them.
They are too concerned
with impressing one another.

Occupied in embracing themselves.

Too busy with obeying The Tree.

But, I swear I heard Him
say to catch me.

The leaves don't notice my descent.

This family will not aid me.

On a frigid Sunday morning,

I fall.

I pray The Tree might save me.

'The First to Fall'

The birds crow a
weeping melody,
trees clean of leaves.

Those crows chirping,
seeing what the branches
have up their sleeves.

Bark peeled back,
showing scars -
lining their arms -
scars placed there
from the wounds
upon their
oaken hearts.

Trees cutting
through the birdsong.
Leaves trampled -
where they belong.

It won't be too long.
They'll be along.
Birds flock to
those branches.
Those crows
know home.

Trees can't
be left alone.
Birds won't leave.

Sapping the sapling's
life - feathers buried into
lumbering decay - leaving
trees in utter dismay.

The birds
always seem to take
my breath away.

'The Birds'

Get tough, kid.
Don't cry, boy.
Grow up, kid.
Be strong, boy.
Be brave,
Be brave.

They made men
with callous hands -
for wives to curse their
callous hearts.

They made men
to feel no pain -
they'll never say
they feel a thing.

They made a mule to
bear a load
- a man is trained to
wear the yoke,
and charge ahead
when life gives goads.

They made a man to
conquer fears -
a brave one
who can show
no tears.

Be a man.
Be strong.
Be tough.
Protect us.
Work hard.
Provide.
Be brave.
Be brave.

Why do you not care about us?

You never show emotions.

You're never really here.

You work all the time.

When you're home,

you're just not here.

Are you listening?

Say something!

Anything!

Hello?

70%

'Be a Man'

They called me resplendent!

                     I was the king of   here
and the king of
           there!

How I'd kill to just be a servant,
one at nowhere or anywhere.

The sun greeted me each morning
 with the kiss of a fellow,
now it's burning my flesh day in and out.

I am the flame,
and the day is the bellows.

I waste away beside my treasures,
the moths consume what the rust doesn't fancy.

My soiled rags, cling to me.

They're becoming of me.

I am becoming them.

We are one.

It aches.

And...

I was a king.

I cannot be rid of the stink.
I wish I could be clean.
It starts to sting,
to be this dirty.
It's a particular kind of hurting.

But I was like a king!

Like a star shining about the rest,
but so…. so much brighter.

Oh, you should've seen me!

You'd have been so impressed.

I've…

I've forgotten what I look like really.

Am I handsome, sir?

Well, could I be?

Spare some coin?

Something to eat?

A smoke maybe?

What was I saying?

I used to be king!

You should have seen me!

Before I became me.

'I Was a King'

I don't know what's wrong
but somethings not quite right.
It's hard to put my finger on it
when both my hands are tied.
I'd tell you all about it,
but my lips are sealed.
I'd speak to all the pain within,
but nothings real.
I wanna say they said that
time would always heal.
I think they meant that we just
live to be revealed.
We revile at the light of day
and shrink away;
we fucking yield.
I'd point it out to you but
both my hands are tied.
You'd probably think that it
was just another lie -
the vices of an empty man;
a hollow life.
If freedom has a price,
can we not buy the lie?
If lies are all we say,
do we deserve the light?
If I broke free today,
who'd take my place tonight?
If all of this is wrong,
why does it feel so right?
We live like we exist
only to satisfy,
we burry one another
just to kill the time,
we look back on the years,
and cannot rectify...
...when we arrive...

I hope you know my hands were tied.

'Freedom'

There's no story
of mighty valor,
no wretched tale
of the Devil's hour.

There's no meaning
to the words you read,
nothing beneath
the ink that bleeds.

There's no reason,
there's no purpose,
there's no worth to
the words that are worthless.

There's no way,
no hidden value,
nothing to gain
from the letters issued.

There's no point,
but it's not dull,
there's no glass,
so it's not quite full.

There's no detail,
no great speeches,
there's no beauty
that'll leave you speechless.

There's no peril,
there's no hero,
I swear to null
it's less than zero.

There's no light,
but it's not dark,
I gotta go cause
I've hit my mark.

'Untitled'

Crows croaked a cacophony,
over the crowd of bullfrogs -
softly cawing as their feathers
burst into flames.
I saw that fire in
your eyes too.
When we were standing among the
lions - just trying to snuff them out - picking at their fur.

       I think the truth was in the middle.

That suns gonna fall apart now.
Maybe both of them.   We'll see.
Maybe we should get inside?
There's smoke on the horizon.
You don't think they started
these fires….
…….right, friend?

Listen close to their calls,
Those crows know.
They're moving away,
like we should.

Like we should have.

You doing alright?

That ash compliments your eyes.
Bright green. Like things used to be.

Speak to the stones,
place them in your pockets.
Unthrown stones are
worth keeping. You know?
A lesson I wish they learned.

You think we were too trusting?
Come now,
I think I heard the sky falling.
Maybe not…
Could've been the frogs cawing.   *'Bizarre'*

She dances on
the Elysian clouds,
gently moving to
the rain's sweet sounds.

The angel begins
to sing along,
a chorus of light,
a radiant song.

The clouds falling down,
over lavender seas,
splatter their song,
onto listening leaves.

Why would this
angel descend for me?

'On the Clouds'

I had a dream
- I fell apart.
I shed my flesh
to show my heart.

I had a dream my
bones made way
to a light within
- a hidden day.

This dawn was
just another way,
another way the
light could say,
the things in me
I ought to say,
…the dark came back
- I couldn't stay.

I awoke to the pain,
to the silence you spoke.
I awoke to the hell,
to the horror I've made.

Now I know that I've paid,
for lies that I've told.
My love, where is the fire,
when the love has grown cold?

I had a dream
that in my wake,
the dreamer made
his last mistake.

So, take my breath,
it's haunting me,
words cannot say,
my apology.

This dream has forged reality.
The pain is rediscovery.
                    I hope you know...   *'I'm So Sorry'*

6 fears 7 because 7 ate 9.

10 informed his family and now 7s doing time.

11s the detective, and he's got no hesitation.

7s looking nervous as he asks her 20 questions.

1 - Why'd you do it?

2 - Did you just lose it?

3 - Was it worth it?

4 - You weren't perfect?

5 - What's your motive?

6 - What's a motif?

7 rolls her eyes,

and she sports and evil grin.

Her heart has been maligned,

and 11 ends like 9.

'7 Breaks'

Maybe I was the spider,

famished... or gluttonous.

I spun my webs over your eyes.

You ought not blame yourself for being blind.

I had you in that snare for a time and a time.

What's a spider to do with such a twisted appetite?

In the end, of course, I only devoured myself.

That was after I was done with you.

Finally, I came to.

I told you I was sorry.

It's entirely unsurprising that you wonder...
    ...if that's simply another web too.

I suppose that's just what spiders do.

How can I prove that I long to be true?

'In the Web'

Those cardinals aligned
in a firing line,
The feathers ignite,
they say they're doing fine.
I expected their wings,
to carry them to the skies.
I'm repulsed as I notice
the hell in their eyes.
The trigger is held,
and the bullets all fly,
but the cardinals now still,
only bleed out with flies.

I'd inquire the truth,
and I'd plunder the lies.
I'd exact my revenge,
but hell,
I don't have time.

And the little one there
in the front row seat,

he just claps his hands
as he washes his feet.

The gunner man weeps,
looking over to me.

And I wipe away tears as
fears wiped away me.

I could say that I saw
the last breath of the peace,
I could lie and say the cardinal's
eyes now finally see.

I won't chastise the children
now painting their cheeks,
I won't scold the old gunner
as he takes aim at me.

Oh, I'd fly away now,
but I've ripped off my wings.

How I'd die to myself,
but I've lived to please me!

The barrel brings hell,
to a cardinal's light.
And as life turns to death,
I guess death turns to life.

'A Perspective of Matter'

The pessimist,
the optimist,
the realist

all sitting around the fire,

as the others doze away to the soft strumming of a ukulele
played by a man with a heart consumed by lust and fear.

Someone I once held near and dear.

I miss you, man.

They'll get along somehow,

perhaps just taking turns by the hour.

Hell, maybe by the minute.

Or they'll leave each other alone when I get home.

One hundred miles south of here.

The sinner is weary of the saint,
the saint scolds the sinner
while the nihilist laughs at them both,
 folding his hands behind his head
and letting the flames lick his feet a bit.

They've been warmed for hours,
but the burn is all he yearns.

That one longs to see the clouds turn to ash,
the others can't determine why.

The selfless empath bickers
with the narcissistic apathetic,
 explaining care that just isn't there.

The dead one rolls his eyes.

Those eyes,
 I'm certain I've mentioned,
 full of flies and wretched lies.

So many friends around that fire…

But I guess it was only ever me, myself and I.

The socially awkward kid,
turning inside to look at the one
 who'd give great speeches,
the talkative one is speechless.

So many pieces of a whole,
warring for dominance within.

Everyday seems to be a guessing game
as to who might win.

I only ever feel like I am anything,

when I look into her eyes.

Otherwise, I am nothing...

Just

'Me, *Myself and I*'

Oh, what I'd give to be that breeze.
The one that carries you.
To be a whisper tickling your ears,
a gentle one to lift your tears,
filling you with hope…
a caress for a broken soul…
How I yearn for that change…
yet another chance…
to linger upon you calmly, every part of you,
for as long as such a thing could.
To quiet those fires inside you…
leaving a smoldering wick and a sincere smile… joy upon
your heart.
I want to hold you that way…
to take your breath away in the right way…

Yet…

Behold…

What am I… really?

I am a hurricane.

'Some Breeze'

Revealing those precious details,
the bind forms faster than the shade.

Cut down the shadows of golden,
where life turns to mockery.

Darkness maddening the light,
driving it to the edge of a soul.

Auroras collapsing in the air,
leaving voids as beacons of nothing.

Tomorrow smoldering with cruelties,
ones that long for today's hope.

That which we offered willingly,
interchanging it for despair.

And, of course, that took you away.
Alas, I am nowhere to be found.

Stand on the horizon, drink the stars.
Lay down the yearning for more.

That notion of eternity rises again,
as a spirit sinks into the faults.

The absence is still keenly felt,
but now the gaps can be refilled.

'Upon a Horizon'

Madness,
neural imbalance teetering on an edge
 that the third eye won't view.

 Seemingly external,
existentially exposing extremities...
that are only ever really an exhausted mind.

Insanity isn't what they say, over and over,
it's more than they perceive it to be,
 but they'll define it as they will.

Another label to wield without a helping hand.
Who are we to have aid in making a stand...
against the talking
hours, the waking nightmares growing beneath our hair?
Throw the dogs a bone,
a madman to a pit, give him some prescriptions to foster
indifference.
 Aftertastes of medicinal wastes, stomping out the next
generations, filling the cells.
Are they not filling hell?
Break us down, load us into the war machine, we'll be
marching when you say when. Artificial dreams, we'll spend
when you say spend.
They'll make pills for that too, friend.
They're always engineering new forms of profiteering,
treading down a population instilled with a lack of fear.

What I'd give to hear his voice...

Yet not a one speaks up. What of it?

 If they did, where would the good be?

 Can you push back against the nature of a beast?

We could tame them at least, gripping them tightly with a
leash, everyone all along longing to be released from the cage
of being free.
Which one is elevated?
This one or that?

Why, I'm so elated as a matter of fact!

Opinionate me.
I swear I'm listening,
to those speaking in my mind,
before the dreams were slain altogether. Forever and Never.

Everything in moderation, yes, they'll moderate everything.

 The damn dream thieves, trampling my child, turning to
instruct me on how to decay properly.
Sound the alarm, we've got some waking, greeting the
realities that they hoped you'd never see.

 It's us versus us. Let's dig the divide together, I'll go first.
 We'll take turns crossing the lines they point out from
behind the white flag clad in crimson.
Not us, they'll feign, but we never asked.
 Dig graves in between little heartbeats, seldom seeing for
the needless glory of the self we crave.

Let's lay the days to waste,
 slaying the things we say by the tongues in two,
cursing the day just like they made us to.

 The little one smiles at the sunset,
 ignorant of the hell that waits upon the years to come,
oblivious to the fires of the future they should be protecting.
Project us to the big screen,
 a miraculous distraction, blue light sleight of hand.
They divine that we will fall under their feet,
where we were all along.
Toil day in and out to build their thrones,
 so when they cast their stones
 they won't have to look us in the eye.
Blank space can certainly be a beautiful thing,
 in a proper head space,
 but a filled page, bursting at the seams,

 it seems to me to be yet another   *'Definition of Insanity'*

Capitalize.

Turn it all to gains.

Silence all the pains.

Top dollar is the bottom line.

Budget in tolerance,

to keep the people at bay.

Stay at large, if you may.

Today breeds a new form of dismay,

an abundance of yesteryear's suffering and rage.

Hold that higher than ever, so they'll divide willingly,

while you reap the benefits, the blood they offer.

Lining coffers with debt and dollars.

Oh, the scoffers! Oh, the coffins!

Give them their benefits, to keep them from lashing out.

It isn't fitting to have them throw a fit.

Division, yes, but absolute indifference.

They'll have their independence,

to bow before their benefactor.

Everything else will seldom matter.

Capitalize.

It's all just matter.

'Make Them Madder'

I never wanted to stir the pot.

I only wanted to flip the table,
changing the scene to break away from the fable.

Needless to say, I was unable.

A man has his reasons.
to hang his head low,
biting his tongue and biding his time,
until it's just right to shatter the lies.

A fitting guise gives courage to the fool,
longing to be wise, perhaps in your eyes...

Well, no matter.

From under the mask,
you'll hear the howling laughter,
one day the wretched sounds of alabaster.

There are voids left unexplored,
shadows implore a day like tomorrow.

And these things will come.

Though first shall come sorrow.

One day, there will be one to seize this,

to crush a mask...

Oh, how they will become...

'Fabled'

That's some corner.

A room full of laughter, slaughtered, some side-splitting one liner.

Great work!   Location, location, location.
Is it fitting?

You jest atop mountains of pain, not to cope
as I self-accuse,
but for what?

Glory?
Here, of all places?

Guide the young man by the ears, don't spare the rod.

Is it really that surprising I hadn't done it?

Would you be surprised to know I've tried?

But you didn't ask, because you didn't care.

And there was no glory to be found with me.

So you left me as you found me,

empty.

You know... I'll be fine.

Strange to consider you a friend...

when you proved to be an enemy.

Old friend, you are the epitome of 'pity me'.

Tsk... Tsk... And I have come to do just that.

'Some Corner'

Radiant swirls of a light that faded
far quicker than they took to form.

My hands long frozen as I reach but cannot grasp.

What would your name have been?

What is it now?

Tears I held, to be the strong one, came suddenly later.

One cannot postpone grief indefinitely.

And I suppose starlight is dead as well.

But you are not numbered among them.

For that I am grateful, that you are higher than those stars.

What shame I carry that you watch me fail!

Little ones, I will hold you yet.

One day, we will reminisce about the day we met.

Your father has not forgotten you.

Your mother longs to carry you again.

Perhaps tomorrow, this will end.

I will reach out to that light,
 and it will never fade,
nor shy away from my grasp.

You are cherished,

you will be cherished then.

'Cherished'

On such a broken plane,

we made a family.

From unlevel, unraveled foundations,

we stacked up pain and suffering,

working tirelessly to ensure that it would never

      fall.

         But it was destined to fall, that tower,

our life, written in cycles, a statistical sadism, a stacking of blades that we named walls.

You know it must come down.

It must come down to be rebuilt.

We cannot...

we will not...

allow it to stand another day.

He deserves more, a foundation of love, a labor that we never received.

Walls of honesty, resistant to crumbling.

A roof over his head isn't enough,

it must be the dreams we encourage,

and it will not be easy.

We were only shown to build the way we know.

So we will learn, to live in love, today...   *'Not Tomorrow'*

There lies a garden, sunken under the keep walls, soaking with the slain, it finds its nourishment in the stain of sweet decay.

Such blooms of change, lapping away at the agony from above as they reach ever downward, carving a path in the darkness that we should walk.

This garden yearns for you.

Petals adorned with the bones of the jesters and court magicians, listen closely for the hollow's laughter. Stop and smell the roses, but know that the cursed hour fast approaches.

The scent of each servant spent, tossed away into the pit about your crown, let it fill you.

You know... you shouldn't be here. Such blooms are for the dead, never meant for the eyes of the living.

Many a fool now grow into fauna so cruel; twisting thorns like smoke rising from embers, strangling whatever they may touch.

You should know that the time is coming.

Listen for the hush, as each leaf bows its head among the dead and damned, the growth will cease for a while. All the lushly arranged branches shall grow ever more still... for the hour has come.

I should've mentioned they favor a feast at midnight.

You shouldn't be here.

They find you quite the sight tonight.

Such blooms of change,
now bear their fangs...
          ...Goodbye.   *'Such Blooms of Change'*

Hide that day from my eyes,
I cannot afford to fix them there again.

Break my line of sight,
have me forget what I am,
if you would.

It isn't ever going to be enough,

is it?

Those times are engraved into my flesh,

I can still see them...
as when they were fresh.

 I suppose I can't afford to forget them,
for she was there among the other side of the blades,

she was there,

dancing in the rain as she bore her own pain.

Is that why we fell for one another?

 Is that why we fell together?

So, I must remember.

For in those wounds, beauty found me,
in those days I was loved,

a carcass caressed,

cold, but so warm were those days.

Little in life is truly bittersweet,

but I can name those memories.

Though now I am the rain,

and   *'The Memories Fade'*

You are here.

That's what it reads...

but, honestly, am I really?

Let's define terms,

you : fucking nothing.

are: simply to be - in second person

here: fucking nowhere.

I'll admit, I think they're mistaken.

I've got to be somewhere, surely.

I'm not here.

And I haven't been there.

Not in forever.

Eventually I will return.

I promised.

Where am I now?

Where was I?

Where am I now?

                    I must be...

                                        'Somewhere, Surely'

Abandoned relics,
echoes of tales
we were never told.

 Eon's caress
on long forgotten, rotten steel.

A heart unused is growing still.

Silent stories,
 inlaid with ferrous dust,
not gold.

A world beneath
the eyes of neglect
 - waiting to be revealed.

Lacking the glimmers of modernity,
 time was handed a brush to make art,
 with a palette of salt and rain.

A masterpiece is made, of vermillion and of pain.

While the others cry out upon seeing decay,

I will laugh out loud - *it reminds me of me.*

'Rust'

Now you meld into them,
ambiguous, congruent with the breakers.
An illustrious allusion to elude me.
That's perfectly fine.
Meticulously, you become them, the very ones that
relinquished the dark.
The sophisticated whispers from mouths of arrogance.
That's perfectly fine.
Subsequently, you fall in among their ranks.
Obligatorily, you become obsolete, to me at least.
That's perfectly fine.
Discern yourself at your own peril,
at your earliest convenience.
Quiet down that pseudo-conscience.
Exhume those exhilarating excuses,
incubating inside those insidious inhibitions.

And tell me another lie.

That's perfectly fine.
I've grown,
all the more accustomed to the hell of your lines.
Regrettably, they're rather redundant, a reduction of reality.
Gaslight me, all through the night, so I can see things clearly.
That's perfectly fine.
Cheers to another bright torch revealing a path that leads to
places where the dead can walk so peacefully and freely.
I'll follow along.
I know every word to that old song.
That's perfectly fine.

It's always been perfectly fine.

I swear I'm okay.

It's all just in my mind anyway.

You aren't real,

you're simply a shadow I have yet to bind.

Trust me, that is   *'Perfectly Fine'*

Everyone is telling time,
counting down the minutes,
but I swear that time counts on me.
That's kinda telling, innit?

People wish they could rewind,
others live and some waste time.
I can be the grains of sand,
falling through my shaking hands.

I can hold the hands of fate,
watch them as they start to break,
tell the minutes what to say,
conform the seconds into me.

They will hear the timeless clock,
It's chiming tune begin to mock.
Pressed for time, the hours fail.
Time will tell, just where they fall.

I have a sense of urgency,
it's comparable to eyes that see,
a tongue that tastes and ears that hear,
this sense breathes moments into years.

'A Sense of Urgency'

When the time comes,
be ready.

If you aren't on a side,
you're an enemy.

Armed to the teeth,
blades sharpened
to make a point.

Cloak and dagger,
rumor has it
this is all they're after.

Fear-mongering mongrels,
chewing peace apart
for a taste of panic.

I feel the manic.

Mimicking hysteria,
laughing all the while,
as the bullets fly
true over the divide.

They don't care who gets hit,
so, every shot is honesty.

Genuinely, they don't give a shit.

Apparently, there's apathy,
behind a mask of empathy.

Smoke and mirrors,
plain to see,
commiserating misery.

'Point Taken'

It's just that you have no idea.
I can tell by your smile.
It's too real.
It's the way your eyes don't have to look away,
because there isn't much pain or shame.
It's the way you are happy,
and you mean it what you say you are.
I'm not saying you don't have struggles.
I'm sure you do...
in your own way.
One of us got a 10 out of 10.
I wonder what you'd score,
how you'd place on that scale...
And I'm not saying that I don't need your help.
I just don't like how you pretend to understand.
It's your demeanor that gives it away.
You read about people like me in books,
and you were fascinated as you had compassion.
I am grateful for that.
Just don't pretend to understand...
to live out those books firsthand.
Not like I had to.
You know...
 I'll have to lie to you too...

though for very different reasons
than why you lied to me.

Please pretend to understand.

Please pretend to care.

Please help me.

What is wrong with me?

Fix me... please...

I can't keep going on like this...

'Shrink'

What does it matter if the glass is

half empty

    or

half full

       ... when I can't swim either way?

Who's to say the cat

is live

or dead

if we're the box in the first place?

Surely,

A tree makes a sound when it falls alone,

but more importantly...

why don't we?

                               'Hypothetically

What can I say?   *Speaking'*

I am twice the man I used to be,

and less than half the man that you deserve.

One of these days you're going to say that I am enough,
like you did today,

but I'll believe it.

Honestly, I can't express just what you're worth.

I could write a million words,

they'd say nothing.

Because you really are my everything.

That's why I have this haunting, sinking feeling...

I showed you dark when you were my light.

I swear, you're my life.

You're the best thing that ever happened to me,

I just feel like I'm the worst thing that ever happened to you.

I know there are things I need to do.

There's love in me I need to prove.

I need to show you, but it's true.

Each day you stay I feel renewed.

'Mrs. Canvas'

I'd take a bullet for you.

But I'd do it for me.

Does that end justify the means?

I think that thought is kind of extraordinary.

I can't possibly be the only one gunning for me.

I'm so stupid,

and so very angry -

a beautiful combination, really.

Sometimes I'm smart,

and so full of peace.

Sometimes I'm nothing,

often, I'm everything.

I'm just something,

anything,

but me...

'I Think'

A toast!

To this family,

broken as we are,

gathered together to celebrate!

…our fuckery.

Drink deeply friends! There's more where that came from.

I want to thank you for sharpening my teeth.

It's so easy, now, to devour everything around me.

And for this tongue of fire, consuming everyone I love!

I couldn't have done it without you.

Hell, maybe I could've.

But I owe you guys for the head start!

Dad, you taught me well,
when things go to hell,
I can just give up.
'Go get milk.'

Mom, you showed me what it means
to have never even tried.

To steal.
To lie.

You taught me the apathy that's shaping me.

I'm fitting that mold.

There's a mold in my soul!

Thanks, Grandma,
for setting me straight.

All those slaps across my face really set into my brain
- I'm afraid to speak out - terrified to ask for help!

Sister, maybe you're like me.
Of course we'll never speak,
so we'll never know,
 you know?

Sarah, thanks for the lesson on disgust.
Preying on a child - sickening.
It's so easy to gag when I see myself!

Thank you all for this!
I find peace in the screaming,
solace when I see bleeding.
It's just a reminder of home.
It's comforting to watch
people break now.
When they do,
I feel alive.

And that reminds me of you.

Cheers!

Another toast!

…….I pissed in the punch.   *'Familial Wounds'*

Pulled in every direction,
seams asunder,
worn from the regrets,
filled to the brim with
negative space,
a man has become

a canvas torn.

She waits,
hoping for a day far off,
doubting it will ever come.
Bearing burdens like blades
inside her heart.
Those knives leave her

a canvas torn.

The world crumbles,
heaps of rubble longing
for healing from a
millennium of disconnection.
A thing of beauty, forlorn.
A garden and a flaming sword,
piles of ash smeared upon
nations sharping their fingers.
It really is

a canvas torn.

We stretch ourselves to tearing,

hoping in whatever we will,

scouring this place for some pitiful

forms of love or caring,

but it isn't enough.

And we know it.

Deep down, we drown in an endless

tide of empty promises,

ones we never heard, but felt

when the clouds rolled over

on a day spent alone.

As we try to survive long enough

to find our way to a surface,

don't we long for home,

sinking into the dark?

We tell them we're well,

while hoping that they'll know

 we're worn.

I think we're all

'A Canvas Torn'

C0000229431

THE GREAT
BOOK OF
NORTH CAROLINA

The Crazy History of North Carolina
with Amazing Random Facts & Trivia

**A Trivia Nerds Guide
to the History of the
United States Vol.9**

BILL O'NEILL

ISBN: 978-1-64845-010-5

DON'T FORGET YOUR
FREE BOOKS

CONTENTS

CHAPTER THREE
NORTH CAROLINA'S INVENTIONS, IDEAS, AND MORE

CHAPTER FOUR

CHAPTER SIX
NORTH CAROLINA'S URBAN LEGENDS,
UNSOLVED MYSTERIES, AND OTHER
WEIRD FACTS! 121

INTRODUCTION

How much do you know about North Carolina?

Sure, you know it's located in the Southeastern U.S., but what else do you *really* know about the state? Do you know why it's called North Carolina? Do you know how the state earned its nickname "The Tar Heel State"?

Do you know what historical events have taken place in the state? Do you know about the famous aviators who made history in Kitty Hawk? Do you know about the most famous pirate who lived and died in North Carolina?

Do you know which famous soda company got its start in North Carolina? Do you know which famous fast food chains started out in the state?

If you've ever wondered these things or more about North Carolina, then you've come to the right spot! This isn't just any book about NC. Here, you'll find fun and interesting stories about the Tar Heel State. It doesn't matter if you live in North Carolina or if you're planning a trip to the state. You're bound to learn something you didn't already know.

North Carolina is a state that's rich in its history and culture. We'll bounce around some as we look at some of the most interesting historical facts about the Tar Heel State. You'll learn more about North Carolina's attractions, inventions, pop culture, sports, and more!

This book is broken up into six easy to follow chapters that will help you learn more about North Carolina. When you've finished with each chapter, you'll find a Q&A so that you can test out your knowledge on what you've just read.

Some of the facts you'll read are surprising. Some of the facts are sad, while others may leave you with goosebumps. But one thing all of these facts have in common is that all of them are interesting. Once you've finished this book, you'll walk away with knowledge that will even impress your history teacher!

This book will answer the following questions:

How did North Carolina get its name?

Why is it known as the "Tar Heel State"?

What happened to the "Lost Colony"?

Which famous pirate was killed in the Outer Banks?

What popular recreational activity was invented in the state?

What soda company got its start in North Carolina?

Which sport originated from the Tar Heel State?

Which NBA legend was raised in North Carolina?

What urban legends haunt the state?

What's the most haunted spot in North Carolina?

And so much more!

CHAPTER ONE

NORTH CAROLINA'S HISTORY AND OTHER FACTS

North Carolina is a state that's located in the Southeastern United States. The state is well-known for its diverse elevations, with points at sea level to the east and the Appalachian Mountain range to the west. Some of the Appalachian Mountains subranges that can be found in North Carolina include the Great Smoky Mountains, Blue Ridge Mountains, and Black Mountains. North Carolina was the 12th state to be admitted into the union. How much do you know about the state's history? Do you know how North Carolina got its name or its state nickname? Do you know which famous pirate died off the coast of North Carolina? Have you heard of North Carolina's "Lost Colony"? To find out the answers to these and other questions, read on!

North Carolina's Capital City is Named After This Explorer

Did you know that Raleigh, North Carolina's capital city, is named after explorer Sir Walter Raleigh?

In 1584, Sir Walter Raleigh was given a charter for today's North Carolina (which also included some of the territory of Virginia at the time). The charter had been granted to him by Elizabeth I in order to create an English colony in America.

Sir Walter Raleigh had established two colonies on the coast of North Carolina during the late 1580s. Neither of the colonies was successful, however, and one even produced one of the biggest mysteries of the country to date.

The Mystery of the Lost Colony Remains Unsolved

Chances are, you may have heard of North Carolina's "The Lost Colony." To date, it remains one of the biggest unsolved mysteries in United States history.

The Roanoke Colony was established by Sir Walter Raleigh on North Carolina's Roanoke Island in 1585. It was England's first attempt at a permanent English colony. Sir Walter Raleigh funded the colony, but he never actually visited it.

Many of the colony's early settlers ended up leaving

within a year, due to a lack of supplies and poor relations with the Native Americans in the area.

John White, who was the colony's governor, arrived in 1587. However, he left for England in late 1587 to get assistance from the English government. Because of the Anglo-Spanish War, White was unable to return to Roanoke until 1590. When White finally made it back to the colony, he discovered that the entire colony had disappeared without a trace. The word "CROATOAN" had been carved into a tree.

There have been several theories on what happened to the colonists. For a long time, it was thought that the colonists had been massacred by local Native American tribes. No bodies were ever discovered, however. Researchers believe that the lack of archeological evidence is due to shoreline erosion. Any bodies or other evidence of the colonists or their dwellings are likely underwater.

Another theory is that the colonists may have had to take shelter with the local tribes due to harsh climate conditions. Nothing could ever prove or disprove this theory, however. There were stories that the Roanoke settlers integrated into tribes and had children with them, but nothing was documented.

In 1998, East Carolina University organized an archeological investigation in the Hatteras Islands, where the Croatan tribe is based. They found several artifacts there, which may or may not have been from

Roanoke Colony. Researchers didn't find conclusive evidence, however.

So, what really did happen to the colonists? Unfortunately, the world may never know.

The First American-Born English Child Lived in the Lost Colony

Did you know that the first child born to English parents in America lived in the "Lost Colony?" Unfortunately, like the rest of the colonists, no one knows what happened to her.

Born in August of 1587, Virginia Dare was named after Virginia, which was where she was born. Her grandfather was John White, the Roanoke Colony governor. White discovered that his granddaughter, who would have been three years old at the time, had disappeared with the other colonists.

A number of places throughout both the United States and North Carolina have been named in Virginia Dare's honor, including Dare County in NC. Dare County includes Roanoke Island.

How North Carolina Got Its Name

Have you ever wondered how North Carolina got its name?

Before you can understand the meaning of "North Carolina," it's important to understand how the state was established to begin with.

The first Europeans to settle in North Carolina were English colonists who had migrated south from Virginia.

In 1663, English King Charles II gave the province, which included both today's North Carolina and South Carolina, to a group of noblemen who were known as the "Lords Noblemen." These men had helped Charles get his position on the throne back three years earlier.

They named the area "Carolina" in honor of King Charles I. The word "Carolina" stems from the Latin word *Caroliinus*, which means "Charles."

Carolina was divided into two separate royal colonies in 1729. This is when "North" was added to the colony's name. The divide happened when seven of the Lords Proprietors chose to sell their land to the Crown.

In 1789, North Carolina was admitted to the union.

North Carolina May Have Been the First State to Declare Its Independence from England

Did you know that North Carolina might have been the first state to declare its independence from England?

It has been said that the then-colony of North Carolina declared its independence from the British Crown in May of 1775 in Charlotte, NC. This is all according to a document called the Mecklenburg Declaration of Independence, which was published in 1819. According to the document, a committee of Mecklenburg County citizens declared independence from England following word of the battle of Lexington.

If the document is accurate (which is often widely debated by historians), it would mean that the Mecklenburg Declaration happened over a year before the United States Declaration of Independence.

Among those who do believe the Mecklenburg Declaration of Independence is authentic, some also believe that North Carolina helped pave the way to the Declaration of Independence and the formation of the United States. It may have set the precedent for other states to follow suit in declaring their independence.

Why North Carolina is Known as the "Tar Heel State"

North Carolina's most popular nickname is the "Tar Heel State." Although it's not known for sure how the state earned its nickname, it's widely believed to be because tar was once one of the state's leading products. But where does the "Heel" in the state's nickname come from? There are thought to be two potential theories, both involving war battles.

According to *Americanisms – Old and New*, which was written by John S. Farmer and published in 1889, there was a battle that involved soldiers from North Carolina and Mississippi. During the battle, the North Carolinian soldiers didn't hold their position. The Mississippi soldiers allegedly said the North Carolinians should have tarred their heels that morning, so they would have been able to "stick" to their position.

However, this isn't the only theory on how North Carolina became known as the Tar Heel State. According to another story by Walter Clark, the state got its nickname when North Carolinian soldiers' supporting column failed to hold their position and they had to fight alone. One of the opposing soldiers, allegedly from the Army of Northern Virginia, supposedly asked if there was any more tar down in North Carolina. One of the soldiers said that "Old Jeff" (Jefferson Davis, President of the Confederate States of America) had bought it all up. The Northern Virginia soldier asked what Old Jeff was going to do with the tar, to which the North Carolinian soldier said he was going to stick it to the Northern Virginia's soldiers' heels so that he stuck better in the next fight.

Although the Tar Heel State is the most well-known nickname for the state of North Carolina, the state has several other popular nicknames, too. These include:

- The Old North State, a nickname it earned due to the Carolina colony divide. It references North Carolina being the older, northern settlement in comparison to South Carolina.

- The Land of the Sky, which comes from a book called *The Land of the Sky* by Frances Tiernan. It refers to the Great Smoky Mountains and the Blue Ridge Mountains. In recent times, Asheville, NC has adopted the nickname as its own.

- The Rip Van Winkle State, a nickname that originates from the story *Rip Van Winkle* by Washington Irving, which does *not* take place in North Carolina. (It takes place in the Catskill Mountains of upstate New York). North Carolina was given the nickname due to a period when it had a "sleepy" economy, while neighboring states' economies were booming.

Of these nicknames, the only one that's still used somewhat frequently is the "Old North State."

America's First Gold Rush Took Place in North Carolina

Have you ever wondered where the first gold rush in America took place? When you think of the Gold Rush, California or even Alaska may be the first states that come to mind. You might be surprised to learn that America's very first Gold Rush actually took place in the Tar Heel State!

It all started out back in 1799 when a young boy by the name of Conrad Reed found a shiny, 17-pound "rock." Not realizing what the rock was made of, his family used the large "rock" as a doorstep. Three years later, Reed's father realized that the rock might actually be of value and discovered that it was gold. This is what jumpstarted gold fever in America.

North Carolina became a golden enterprise, drawing in many tourists who wanted to find gold of their own.

Today, you can visit Reed Gold Mine, which is located in Midland, North Carolina. The gold mine is a national historic landmark today. There you can explore the underground mining tunnels that were at the forefront of the first Gold Rush.

North Carolina is Home to "The Graveyard of the Atlantic"

Did you know that North Carolina's Outer Banks is known as "The Graveyard of the Atlantic"?

The Outer Banks earned this nickname because there have been so many shipwrecks in the area, with estimates ranging from hundreds to thousands. There have been so many sunken ships in the area due to so many hurricanes in the area, as well as the

Gulf Streams and Labrador Currents meeting.

These shipwrecks have been happening ever since the 1500s, up until World War II.

There have been more than 500 sunken ships in Cape Hatteras alone, which is why it's home to the Graveyard of the Atlantic Museum.

Many of the shipwrecks in the area can still be seen to this day. The Crystal Coast is a popular spot for people to explore the sunken ships.

Famous Pirate Blackbeard Died in the Outer Banks

Did you know that Blackbeard, one of the most famous pirates in the entire world, was killed in the Outer Banks?

Blackbeard, whose real name was Edward Teach, came from Bristol, England. He originally served as a privateer during the Queen Anne's War, working for the British Government to attack and plunder enemy merchant ships. When the war ended in 1714, Teach became a pirate.

In 1717, Teach commandeered a ship, which he named "Queen Anne's Revenge," and got a crew for himself. He began plundering ships off the Carolina and Virginia coasts.

One of his most well-known expeditions took place

in Charleston, South Carolina, where he captured a number of prominent citizens. He held them for ransom until the city agreed to pay him in medical supplies. Teach quickly became known as one of the most dangerous pirates of his time.

It was also at that point in time that he began to go by his infamous nickname, "Blackbeard." The nickname came about because Blackbeard would dress in black and twist his wild beard into wisps. He would stick lighted matches under his hat and around his face to give himself a ghostly appearance that would light up his wild eyes. This tactic was to scare his victims, who often saw him as the "face of the devil." Most ships surrendered to him instead of attempting to fight him, simply due to his frightening appearance.

When Blackbeard wasn't at sea, he was generally on the coast and inland communities of North Carolina. He lived in Bath, North Carolina. Ocracoke Island and the surrounding region provided a perfect hiding spot for him, and he spent many years plundering ships and holding hostages for ransom in the region.

Blackbeard's not the only pirate who caused a ruckus in the Outer Banks. Other pirates, including Calico Jack, Mary Reed, and Anne Bonney, also frequented the area. The reason is simple: Ocracoke Island and nearby Portsmouth Island were two of the biggest ports for goods in the area. North Carolina was also a big draw to pirates because the state didn't have a strict government policy on piracy. Charles Eden, who was the Governor of the state, was believed to ignore pirate activity along the Carolina coast. Eden and Blackbeard were neighbors and rumor has it that they were also friends.

With the governor ignoring the problem, the citizens of North Carolina sought help from Alexander Spotswood, the Governor of Virginia. Governor Spotswood commissioned a crew of British Naval Officers. Under the lead of Lt. Robert Maynard, they traveled to Ocracoke Island to capture Blackbeard.

In November of 1718, the crew located Blackbeard off the coast of Ocracoke Island. The crew and Blackbeard fought in what would be the pirate's last battle.

Blackbeard was killed after being shot 5 times. Maynard allegedly cut off the pirate's head and hung it from the bow of his ship as they sailed back to Virginia, in proof of the crew's defeat.

The inlet where Blackbeard was killed is known today as "Teach's Hole." It's home to a museum exhibiting the legendary pirate's life and death.

Although Blackbeard was only a pirate for a couple of years, his mark as one of the most infamous pirates in history lives on.

North Carolina Was the Last State to Join the Confederacy

You probably already know that North Carolina was a part of the Confederacy during the American Civil War. But do you know what led the state to be the last to join the Confederacy?

By 1860, North Carolina was known as a slave state. One-third of the state's population at the time were slaves. This may seem like a lot, but this was actually a smaller number that many of the other Southern states.

North Carolina was the last state to join the Confederacy. The state made the decision only after Abraham Lincoln had requested on it to invade its sister state, South Carolina, in 1861. North Carolina being the last state to join the Confederacy has widely been disputed, with some claiming that Tennessee was the last to join. However, Tennessee informally seceded from the U.S. on May 7th, while North Carolina formally seceded on May 20th.

Although North Carolina was the last state to join the Confederacy, the state's mark on the war was a significant one.

For starters, North Carolinian Private Henry Wyatt became the first Confederate soldier to be killed in the Civil War in June of 1861. His death happened during the Battle of Big Bethel.

The state also holds the record of the highest number of Confederate soldiers killed over the course of the American Civil War. An estimated 20,000 North Carolinian soldiers were killed during the war, which is more than any other Confederate state. Another 20,000 soldiers from North Carolina also died as the result of diseases in the Civil War.

The First Flight Happened in the Tar Heel State

Did you know that the first flight took place in North Carolina?

The Wright Brothers, Orville and Wilbur Wright, made the first successful powered flight in Kitty Hawk, North Carolina in 1903. They tested several prototypes at the location, which was remote enough to provide them with privacy, soft grounds, and steady winds.

Their heavier-than-air flying machine, which they called the Wright Flyer, allowed the pilot to steer the aircraft effectively and maintain its equilibrium. This method continues to be the standard technology on fixed-wing aircraft to this day.

The Wright Brothers' technology differed from the other experimenters at the time, who focused more on developing a powerful engine.

The Wrights used a small homebuilt wind tunnel in

their invention. They also successfully designed and built wings and propellers that were more efficient than any other prototypes that came before them.

Today, North Carolina license plates boast the claim that the state was "First in Flight." Ohioans are often disputing this claim, however. They argue that the Wright Brothers actually had their first flight in Ohio, where the brothers lived and first began designing their invention. While it's widely believed that the brothers likely did test their first prototype out in Ohio, their first successful flight—and their most famous flight—took place in Kitty Hawk.

The Outer Banks Has Its Own Dialect

Many states throughout the country have their own dialects. It might surprise you to learn that the Outer Banks and Pamlico Sound regions of North Carolina have their own dialect.

The dialect is formally known as the Ocracoke Brogue. Known less formally as the "Hoi Toider," High Tider is a dialect of the English language. However, the dialect is so thick that it's difficult for English speakers to be able to decipher it easily. Although the dialect's vocabulary, grammar, and punctuation can all be traced to Southwestern England, Higher Tider sounds like a language all its own.

The dialect allegedly started out during the 1600s. It stayed around for many generations because people from the Outer Banks tended to stay on their islands and were isolated from outsiders (who are known as "dingbatters" in High Tider). The dialect is dying today, however. There are said to be only about 150 speakers of the dialect remaining.

North Carolina is Home to Some Unique Wildlife

How much do you know about North Carolina's plants and wildlife? Do you know about the unique species that call the state home?

In the city of Brevard, NC, there's a population of white squirrels—not to be mistaken for albino squirrels. Rumor has it that two white squirrels escaped from a fair that passed through Brevard during the 1940s and continued to breed. While it's unknown if this is true or not, the white squirrels do call the town their home.

There are also blue ghost fireflies that can be found in North Carolina. Unlike the fireflies that are found throughout the rest of the United States, which flash light yellow, these fireflies flash a blue-green shade. These lightning bugs are becoming less frequently seen throughout the state, but they can still be found at DuPont State Recreational Forest, which is located near Cedar Mountain.

The Venus Fly Trap is also native to Hampstead, North Carolina. The only states in the country where the plant can be found are North Carolina and South Carolina.

Two Nuclear Bombs Were Accidentally Dropped in North Carolina

Did you know that a major catastrophe was once diverted in North Carolina?

Back in 1961, two nuclear bombs were dropped on Goldsboro, North Carolina. The bombs, which were dropped on accident, were believed to more than 250 times more powerful than the bomb that was dropped on Hiroshima.

One of the bombs was even activated when it was dropped. Fortunately, it didn't explode thanks to an emergency kill switch, which was incredibly lucky. The kill switch was often faulty.

Three Former United States Presidents Have Hailed from the State

Did you know that three former United States Presidents came from the Tar Heel State?

Andrew Jackson, who was born in Waxhaw Settlement (on the border of North Carolina and South Carolina), was the country's 7th president. He served from 1829 to 1837. Prior to becoming president,

Jackson got famous as a United States Army General and also served in both Congressional houses.

James K. Polk was the 11th President of the United States. Polk was born in Pineville, North Carolina. He went on to serve as Speaker of the House of Representatives and the Governor of Tennessee before serving as president between the years of 1845 and 1849.

Andrew Johnson was the 17th President of the United States. Born in Raleigh, Johnson became president after serving as Vice President to Abraham Lincoln until the time of his assassination in 1865.

Although no presidents have been from the state since the 1800s, former U.S. Senator John Edwards ran for vice president along Senator John Kerry in 2004 and president in 2008. Edwards was not elected into office during either of those elections, however.

RANDOM FACTS

1. North Carolina has the 9th highest population of all the U.S. states. In 2018, it was estimated that the population of North Carolina was around 10.3 million. In terms of geographic area, the state ranks at No. 28, with a total land area of 53,819 square miles.

2. Charlotte is the most populated municipality in North Carolina. It's also the 20th largest city in all of the United States. Additionally, Charlotte is the 2nd largest banking center in America, surpassed only by New York City. Charlotte is home to Bank of America and Wachovia headquarters.

3. Research Triangle Park is the largest research park in America. The word "Triangle" in the park's name comes from the three cities and, more importantly, the three research universities in the area: North Carolina State University in Raleigh, Duke University in Durham, and the University of Carolina at Chapel Hill.

4. North Carolina is home to the oldest public university in America! The University of North Carolina-Chapel Hill, which was founded in 1798, is the oldest public university in the

country. The first student on the UNC campus was Hinton James, who enrolled at the university in February of 1795. Rumor has it that James walked 162 miles from Wilmington to Chapel Hill. It allegedly took him two weeks to get there. By the end of 1795, the university had enrolled 41 students, who were taught by two professors.

5. North Carolina is the biggest producer of sweet potatoes in the country. More than 50% of the country's sweet potatoes are grown in central to eastern North Carolina each year.

6. North Carolina is a big producer of the country's Christmas trees. Approximately 15 to 20 percent of the country's real Christmas trees are produced in the Tar Heel State each year. The North Carolina Fraser fir is commonly grown in the state.

7. North Carolina is the only state in America that has 100 counties. While it's not the state with the highest number of counties (that would be Texas, which has 254), it is the only state that can say it has 100.

8. It has been estimated that North Carolina is hit by a hurricane almost every four years (or 3.44 years, to be exact).

9. North Carolina ranks at No. 3 in terms of hurricane frequency. The state has been directly hit with 47 hurricanes since 1851. The only states

to be hit with more hurricanes than North Carolina are Florida and Louisiana.

10. Craft beer is a booming business in Asheville, North Carolina. The city has the largest number of brewers per capita, in comparison to any other city in America. Wicked Weed Brewing, Green Man Brewery, and Highland Brewing Company are a few of the city's most well-known breweries.

11. The state song is "The Old North State," the cardinal is the state bird, milk is the state beverage, and the state motto is *Esse quam videri*, which in English means, "To be, rather than to seem."

12. Hiram Rhoades Revels, who was born in Fayetteville, NC, was the first ever African-American member of U.S. Congress. Revels, who was a Mississippi Republican Senator, was first elected into office in 1871.

13. North Carolina's highway system has over 77,000 miles of roads, making it the largest state-maintained highway system in the country.

14. North Carolina is known for its beautiful lakes and streams. The state is home to 1,500 lakes spanning 10 acres or more in size, as well as 37,000 miles of freshwater streams.

15. Just like every other state, North Carolina has a

number of strange laws. Bingo games may not last more than five hours (and alcohol cannot be served at them), a three-dollar tax must be paid on all "white goods" sold in the state, and it's illegal to sing off-key. Stealing more than $1,000 worth of grease will earn you a felony. It's not legal to be a professional fortune teller, but you can practice as an amateur fortune teller *only* at a school or church. It's illegal to use elephants to plow cotton fields. The state also has a number of weird sexual laws: it's illegal to have sex in a churchyard, take part in oral sex, have the blinds open or take part in any position other than the missionary position. If you're a couple who's staying overnight in a hotel, there must be double beds spaced two feet apart. If you aren't married and register yourself as a married couple at a hotel, state law says you're now legally married. Your marriage can also be declared void if either partner is physically impotent.

16. Native Americans inhabited North Carolina long before the Europeans arrived in the region. Some of the Native American tribes that could be found throughout North Carolina included the Cape Fear Indians, Catawba, Cherokee, Pamlico, Roanoke, and Waxhaw.

17. North Carolina is the leading producer of tobacco of any U.S. state, growing almost 375 million pounds of tobacco every year. The state's tobacco

production is double that of Kentucky, which ranks at No. 2 in terms of U.S. tobacco production.

18. Twenty of the largest emeralds to ever be found in the United States were found in North Carolina. One of them, which is the largest emerald to ever be found in North America to date is the "Carolina Emperor," which is 64.83 carats.

19. North Carolina was the first state to receive news of the Titanic sinking in 1912. The United States Weather Station in Hatteras Village was the first to receive the distress telegraph from the Titanic letting them know about the tragedy.

20. Charlie Brown, who was a Charlotte native, was one of only 12 people who has ever walked on the moon.

Test Yourself – Questions

1. North Carolina was named in honor of:

    a. Sir William Raleigh
    b. Charles IX of France and then Charles I and Charles II of England
    c. South Carolina

2. Which former U.S. President was <u>not</u> from North Carolina?

    a. Richard Nixon
    b. Andrew Jackson
    c. Andrew Johnson

3. The famous pirate who died in North Carolina was:

    1. William Kidd
    2. Anne Bonny
    3. Thomas "Blackbeard" Teach

4. North Carolina ranks at what No. in terms of the U.S.'s most populous states?

    a. No. 3
    b. No. 10
    c. No. 9

5. The Venus Fly Trap can only be found in North Carolina and which other state?

    a. Georgia
    b. Virginia
    c. South Carolina

Answers

1. b.

2. a.

3. c

4. c.

5. b.

CHAPTER TWO
NORTH CAROLINA'S POP CULTURE

How much do you know about North Carolina's pop culture? Do you know what celebrities are from the Tar Heel State? Do you know which movies or shows have been set and/or filmed in North Carolina? Have you heard about the abandoned cotton mill village where one popular movie series was filmed? Do you know which city is known for its booming film industry? Do you know which '90s R&B duo was from the state? Have you heard about one country music legend's troubled adolescence in North Carolina? Do you know which author set all of his books, many of which have been converted into films, in the Tar Heel State? Read on to learn more about North Carolina's pop culture!

North Carolina Has Been Called the "Hollywood of the East"

Did you know that North Carolina has been referred to as the "Hollywood of the East"? You may be surprised to learn that North Carolina actually has a booming film industry!

Wilmington, North Carolina is home to EUE Screen Gems Studio, the largest TV and movie production studio outside of California. The studio's soundstage, "Dream Stage 10," is the 3rd largest soundstage in the United States. It's also home to America's largest special effects water tank.

EUE Screen Gems Studio opened back in 1984. Since then, the following major motion pictures have been filmed at the studio:

- *28 Days*
- *A Walk to Remember*
- *Blue Velvet*
- *Black Knight*
- *Cape Fear*
- *Empire Records*
- *Hounddog*
- *Iron Man 3*
- *Nights in Rodanthe*
- *Teenage Mutant Ninja Turtles*
- *The Crow*
- *We're the Millers*

A number of TV shows have also been filmed at the studio, including:

- *Dawson's Creek*
- *One Tree Hill*
- *Under the Dome*

Since Wilmington has been at the heart of America's film industry, the city itself has been referred to as "Wilmywood," a combination of "Wilmington" and "Hollywood."

North Carolina Has Been the State with the Most Contestants on This Singing Competition Show

Did you know that the Tar Heel state has produced more *American Idol* contestants than any other state in the country?

Some of the most notable contestants from North Carolina who have been on the singing competition show include:

- Chris Daughtry (hometown: Roanoke Rapids, North Carolina).
- Kellie Pickler (hometown: Albemarle, North Carolina).
- Fantasia Barrino (hometown: High Point, North Carolina).
- Clay Aiken (hometown: Raleigh).
- Scotty McCreery (hometown: Garner, North Carolina).

31

- Bucky Covington (hometown: Rockingham, North Carolina).

This Popular Movie Was Filmed in North Carolina

This movie grossed $694 million across the world and set records with a $67.3 at the box office on opening day. Did you know that the film *The Hunger Games*, which is based on the book series by Suzanne Collins, was filmed in North Carolina?

Henry Mill Village—an abandoned cotton mill village near Asheville, North Carolina—served as District 12 in the film. You can take a tour of Henry Mill Village's film spots through the Hunger Games Unofficial Fan Tours. Included in the tour are an archery workshop/lesson, a behind-the-scenes look at film spots, re-enactments of scenes from the film, and a lunch that includes food from the film/book. You can also visit Katniss Everdeen's house from the film and the Company Store, which acted as Mellark's Bakery in *The Hunger Games.*

Dupont State Forest served as the arena in the first movie in *The Hunger Games* series. There, you'll find tour guides, who can show you some of the spots that were used in the film. You can also swim in the same water from the movie.

This *Hunger Games* Actress is from the Tar Heel State

Did you know that actress Julianne Moore, who played President Alma Coin in *The Hunger Games: Mockingjay – Part 1* & *2*, is from North Carolina?

Moore was born at North Carolina's Fort Bragg army installation. She was born with the name "Julie Anne Smith."

Her father was a paratrooper during the Vietnam War, later earning the rank of colonel. For this reason, Smith's family moved around often before eventually moving to Frankfurt, Germany. It was there that she began acting at the school. Her English teacher encouraged her to pursue a career in acting. Her parents insisted that she earn a college degree so she'd have a back-up plan, so she attended Boston University, where she earned a BFA in Theatre.

After graduation, Smith moved to New York and registered her stage name with the Actors' Equity. She began to perform with off-Broadway theatre. In 1985, she earned a part in an episode of the soap opera *The Edge of Night*. The same year, her big break came when she became a regular cast member on the soap opera *As the World Turns*, in which she played the double role of half-sisters Frannie and Sabrina Hughes. In 1988, she won a Daytime Emmy Award for the roles.

Moore continued to earn a number of TV roles. Her next big break came when she landed the roles in *Nine Months* and *The Lost World: Jurassic Park*. This led her to be a top Hollywood actress.

She later went on to play in a number of other movies, including *The Big Lebowski, Magnolia, Hannibal, The Kids Are All Right,* and *Crazy, Stupid, Love*. She also played Sarah Palin in the made-for-TV movie *Game Change*, for which she won awards. She won Academy Award for her role as an Alzheimer's patient in the film *Still Alice* and also earned a Best Actress award at the Cannes Film Festival for her role in *Maps to the Stars*. After she played President Coin in *The Hunger Games* film series, she went on to play in the movie *Kingsman: The Golden Circle*

Julianne Moore has also authored a children's book series about a girl named "Freckleface Strawberry."

And to think that it all started out in Fort Bragg, North Carolina!

A Classic Romance Movie Was Also Filmed in the Tar Heel State

Did you know that North Carolina served as a backdrop in the movie *Dirty Dancing*, starring Patrick Swayze and Jennifer Grey?

Although scenes from the film were also shot at the Mountain Lodge in Pembroke, Virginia, Lake Lure in

North Carolina was where some of the movie's most iconic scenes were filmed.

The dance on the log was filmed at Lake Lure. The stone stairs where Baby practiced her steps and carried watermelons also still stand, though they are now private property and not accessible to the public.

If you want to spot all of the film locations from Lake Lure, you can even take a guided tour with the Lake Lure Tours Boat Company.

This Iconic Actress Was From North Carolina

Today, she's considered one of America's most iconic classic actresses, often compared to Marilyn Monroe and Audrey Hepburn. But did you know that the late Ava Gardner's life started out in North Carolina?

Ava Gardner was born near Grabtown, North Carolina, where she was the youngest of seven children. When she was seven, Gardner's family moved to Newport News, Virginia. When she was 15, her father died from bronchitis, leading the family to move to Rock Ridge, North Carolina. Ava Gardner graduated from Rock Ridge High School in 1939. She later went to attend Atlantic Christian College in Wilson, North Carolina, where she took secretarial classes.

In 1941, Gardner's life took a turn for stardom when she was visiting her sister Beatrice in New York City. Beatrice was married to a man named Larry Tarr, who was a professional photographer. While Ava was visiting, Tarr took her portrait. Satisfied with the results, Larry displayed it in the front window of Tarr Photography Studio, which was located on Fifth Avenue. It drew the attention of Barnard Duhan, a Lowes Theaters legal clerk who pretended to be an MGM talent scout to meet women. Duhan tried (unsuccessfully) to get Ava Gardner's number and also commented that someone should send MGM her info. Tarr's sent her information to MGM right away.

MGM's New York talent department wanted to meet with Ava Gardner. She had already returned to North Carolina for college and traveled back to New York for the interview. The rest is history! Ava Gardner was offered a contract with MGM and left school to set out on her Hollywood career in 1941.

MGM did provide Ava Gardner with a speech coach, as they were unable to understand her North Carolina accent.

In 1946, after several small roles, Gardner had her first hit with the film *The Killers*, in which she played femme fatale, Kitty Collins.

Her most notable role was as Maria Vargas in the film *The Barefoot Contessa*, alongside Humphrey Bogart.

Gardner also played Guinevere in the *Knights of the Round Table* in 1953, in which she co-starred with Robert Taylor.

And to think it all started out in Grabtown, North Carolina!

This Alternative Rock Band Was Formed in North Carolina

Did you know the alternative rock band Ben Folds Five was formed in North Carolina?

Ben Folds Five was formed in Chapel Hill back in 1993 by the band's frontrunner, Ben Folds. Even though their name might lead you to believe that there were five members, there were only ever three because they thought it sounded better than "Ben Folds Three."

The band's members include Ben Folds who does vocals, piano, keyboards, and most of the band's songwriting. Robert Sledge does backup vocals and plays the bass guitar, double bass, and synthesizer, while Darren Jessee also does backup vocals and songwriting and plays drums and percussion.

The band released their first song "Underground" in 1995, but it wasn't until 1997 when they had their biggest success with the single "Brick" from their 2nd album. Although the group identifies as alternative rock, they also had some mainstream success in the pop music scene. Their music is known to have a "punk" feel to it.

Ben Folds Five also did a cover of the Steely Dan

song "Barrytown" for the *Me, Myself, & Irene* movie soundtrack.

The band broke up in October of 2000.

As a solo artist, Ben Folds went on to release a number of popular singles, with the most well-known being "The Luckiest."

Ben Folds Five reunited in 2011 and released their 4th album, *The Sound of the Life of the Mind*, in 2012.

This '90s R&B Duo is From North Carolina

Did you know that '90s R&B duo K-Ci and JoJo is from Wingate, North Carolina?

The brothers, whose real names are Cedric "K-Ci" Hailey and Joel "JoJo" Hailey, originally started out as part of the R&B group Jodeci. By 1994, K-Ci and JoJo began to embark on their journey as a duo. They did the song "How Could You" for the movie *Bulletproof*, which starred Adam Sandler and the Wayans Brothers. They were later featured in 2Pac's song "How Do U Want It."

Today, they're most well-known for their No. 1 *Billboard* Hot 100 hit "All My Life," which was a popular wedding song when it came out. They also received a lot of recognition for their song "Crazy," which was featured on the *Save the Last Dance* soundtrack and hit No. 3 on the *Billboard* Hot 100.

Fun Fact: K-Ci & JoJo are cousins with *American Idol* winner Fantasia Barrino.

This Legendary Singer and Civil Rights Activist Was from the Tar Heel State

Did you know that Nina Simone was from North Carolina? The late singer was known for her music, as well as her involvement as an activist in the Civil Rights Movement.

Simone was given the name Eunice Kathleen Waymon when she was born in Tryon, North Carolina. She was born into a poor family as the sixth of eight children.

When she was just three years old, Waymon began to learn how to play the piano. The first song she learned to play was "God Be With You, Till We Meet Again." She played at her local church, but she didn't have her first classic recital concert until she was 12 years old. Since her parents were African-American, they were forced to move to the back of the hall so that white people could sit in the front. She refused to perform until her parents were moved back to the front of the hall. Later in life, Nina Simone attributed that incident to her role as a Civil Rights Movement activist.

Waymon's music teacher helped establish a fund that would allow her to attend Allen High School for

Girls in Asheville, North Carolina. After she graduated from high school in 1950, Simone attended the Julliard School of Music. She was a student of Carl Friedberg. She auditioned for Curtis Institute of Music in Philadelphia, where she had applied for a scholarship. Even though her audition was well-received, her application was rejected. She believed that her rejection had been a result of racial discrimination. Days before she died in 2003, the Curtis Institute of Music granted her an honorary degree.

Eunice Waymon came up with the stage name "Nina Simone." She came up with the name to disguise her music from her family members because she had chosen to play "the devil's music" (or "cocktail piano") at an Atlantic City nightclub to make money. That nightclub is also what started Simone's career as a jazz vocalist. She was told she had to sing to her own piano piece.

Simone went on to record over 40 albums during the course of her career. Her 1958 song "I Loves You, Porgy" was a hit in the U.S.

Her musical style was a combination of jazz, soul, R&B, gospel, pop, and classical.

And it all started out in Tryon, North Carolina!

All of This Author's Novels Are Set in North Carolina

Did you know every single one of Nicholas Sparks' books, many of which have been adapted to film, are set in North Carolina?

Here's a list of some of the author's books and the towns in which they were set:

- *The Notebook* – The author's first and most famous novel is set in New Bern, which is where Nicholas Sparks himself lives. The book inspired the film of the same name, which stars Ryan Gosling and Rachel McAdams as Noah and Allie.

- *The Wedding* – The sequel to *The Notebook* is also set in New Bern, NC.

- *A Bend in the Road* – This novel is also set in New Bern, North Carolina.

- *Message in a Bottle* – This novel, which inspired the movie adaptation that featured Kevin Costner and Robin Wright, was set in Wilmington, North Carolina.

- *A Walk to Remember* – This book was set in Beaufort, North Carolina. The film adaptation included Mandy Moore and Shane West as Jamie and Landon.

- *Dear John* – The novel that inspired the movie starring Channing Tatum and Amanda

Seyfried was set in Wilmington, North Carolina.

- *The Choice* – This novel was set in Wilmington, North Carolina. Benjamin Walker and Teresa Palmer starred in the film adaptation.

- *The Last Song* – Set in Wrightsville Beach, North Carolina, this novel is unique because Nicholas Sparks first wrote the movie script and later wrote the book. He wrote it for Miley Cyrus, who wanted to star in a movie similar to *A Walk to Remember*. Unlike the book, the movie is set in Georgia. It's the only Nicholas Sparks movie to be set in Georgia, in fact. Liam Hemsworth played alongside Cyrus in the film adaptation.

- *The Rescue* – This novel was set in Edenton, North Carolina.

- *See Me* – This novel was set in Wilmington, North Carolina.

- *Nights in Rodanthe* – Set in Rodanthe, the film adaptation of this novel featured Richard Gere and Diane Lane. It's the only one of Nicholas Sparks' novels to actually have the location in the title.

- *The Guardian* – This novel was set in Swansboro, North Carolina.

- *Safe Haven* – This film was set in Southport, North Carolina. Some of the scenes from the film, which stars Julianne Hough and Josh Duhamel, were filmed in Southport.

- *The Best of Me* – Set in Oriental, North Carolina, the film adaptation starred James Marsden and Michelle Monaghan.
- *The Longest Ride* – This novel, which was set in Black Mountain, North Carolina, was adapted into a film starring Britt Robertson and Scott Eastwood.
- *Two by Two* – This book was set in Charlotte, North Carolina.
- *Every Breath* – This novel was set in Sunset Beach, North Carolina.

Three more of Nicholas Sparks' novels were set in fictional towns in North Carolina. These include *The Lucky One, At First Sight,* and *True Believer.* Sparks has said that *True Believer* was, in part, inspired by the legend of the Brown Mountain Lights of Western North Carolina.

Since Sparks lives in North Carolina and has set all of his books in the state, one might assume that the novelist was born in the state. You'd be wrong, however. Nicholas Sparks was actually born and grew up in Omaha, Nebraska!

This North Carolina Town Inspired a Fictional Town in This Hit Show

Did you know that Mount Airy, North Carolina was the inspiration behind the town of Mayberry in the hit 1960s sitcom *The Andy Griffith Show*?

Andy Griffith himself was born and raised in Mount Airy, NC. The late actor attended Mount Airy High School and the University of North Carolina at Chapel Hill. Although Griffith originally studied to become a Moravian preacher, he instead graduated with a B.A. in Music.

Following graduation, Griffith taught music and drama at Goldsboro High School in North Carolina for a few years.

Griffith later went on to act, first rising to fame with his role in the movie *A Face in the Crowd* before being offered the role of Andy Taylor in *The Andy Griffith Show*, which aired for eight years.

Today, the town of Mount Airy memorializes Andy Griffith and the show. You can visit the Andy Griffith Museum, Griffith's childhood home, and some of the local shops that were featured in *The Andy Griffith Show*. You'll also find bronze statues of Andy and Opie (played by Ron Howard) in the town.

Even though Andy Griffith passed away in 2012, his hometown still keeps his memory and legacy alive.

There's an annual festival called "Mayberry Days" that's held in Mount Airy each year in honor of the actor and his most famous sitcom.

This Rock and Roll Hall of Famer Was Raised in NC

Did you know that Rock and Roll Hall of Famer James Taylor was raised in North Carolina? The five-time Grammy Award-winning singer was born in Boston, but his family moved to Chapel Hill when he was just a toddler.

Taylor, who was inducted in the Rock and Roll Hall of Fame back in 2000, is one of the best-selling musicians in history. The artist has sold more than 100 million records worldwide.

James Taylor attended public primary school in Chapel Hill. While he was growing up in North Carolina, Taylor learned how to play the cello as a child. By the age of 12, he switched to playing the guitar. His guitar style is said to have been influenced by the music of Woody Guthrie, along with hymns and carols. He also experimented with his sister's keyboards.

Taylor started Milton Academy, a preparatory boarding school in Massachusetts when he was 13. When his family was on summer vacation in Martha's Vineyard, he made friends with Danny

Kortchmar, an aspiring guitarist who recognized what a good singer Taylor was. When he was 14, Taylor wrote his first song on the guitar. A couple of years later, Taylor and Kortchmar started playing at coffeehouse around Martha's Vineyard. They called themselves "Jamie & Kootch."

After returning to Milton Academy and spending some time in McLean Hospital in Belmont, Massachusetts for depression, Taylor headed to New York City where he started a band called the Flying Machine. Unfortunately, Taylor fell into using heroin during that time, though the band did record a song called "Rainy Day Man"—a song that Taylor would later rerecord for his solo album.

When Taylor moved to London to start a solo career, his friend Danny Kortchmar helped connect him to Peter Asher, who worked for the Beatles' record label, Apple Records. Taylor gave Asher a demo, which included his song "Something in the Way She Moves." Demo played it for Paul McCartney and George Harrison. They were impressed, and Taylor was the first non-British act to be signed to Apple Records.

James Taylor got his big break in 1970 with his single "Fire and Rain," which peaked at No. 3 on the *Billboard* Hot 100. In 1971, his single "You've Got a Friend" reached No. 1.

He's also well-known for his cover of the song "How Sweet It Is (To Be Loved by You).

This Country Music Legend Had a Troubled Past Growing Up in NC

There are a number of country singers who have come from North Carolina, but Randy Travis is, by far, the most significant country musician to come from the state. Did you know that Travis was born in Marshville, North Carolina? Though Travis has had a lot of success in the music industry, it might surprise you to learn that the singer's life got off to a rocky start.

Born as Randy Traywick, the singer started playing the guitar and singing in his church's choir when he was just eight years old. He and his brother started an act as a duo. They called themselves the "Traywick Brothers" and performed locally. Travis, who fought often with his father, dropped out of high school. He soon became a juvenile delinquent. Some of his offenses included auto theft and burglary.

By 1975, however, Travis earned a job as both a singer and cook a nightclub called County City USA in Charlotte, North Carolina. At the time, his brother had been serving time in prison for a high-speed car chase. The owner of the club, Elizabeth Hatcher, became fond of Randy Travis. When Travis had another run-in with the law, the judge told him that he would be doing a lot of jail time if he didn't turn his life around. Travis was released into Hatcher's custody.

In addition to being his legal guardian, Elizabeth Hatcher also became Travis's manager. Together, they began to focus on his singing career.

Randy Travis recorded his first album under his real name, with his first album being titled *Randy Traywick*. One of the songs from the album, "She's My Woman," reached No. 91 on the *Billboard* Hot Country Songs chart.

Travis moved in with Elizabeth Hatcher, which put a lot of strain on her marriage. She eventually left her husband and moved to Nashville with Travis. The two formed a romantic relationship.

In 1982, Randy was given an album deal with Warner Bros. Records. Part of the contract was that he must perform under the stage name of Randy Travis and he also had to keep his relationship with Hatcher a secret.

Eventually, their relationship did become public and they married in 1991. They remained married for 19 years before divorcing—and ending their business contract—in 2010.

Since his career took off, Randy Travis has had 50

singles that have hit the *Billboard* Hot Country Songs charts. Of those, 16 have peaked at No. 1.

Known for his distinctive baritone voice, Travis's neotraditional style has made him a major figure in the country music industry since he rose to fame during the 1980s.

Travis's music began to decline on the charts during the mid-1990s. He has since begun to focus more on Christian music. In addition to his music career, Randy Travis has also pursued acting. He starred in the movie *The Rainmaker* in 1997 alongside Matt Damon, in *Black Dog* with Patrick Swayze in 1998, and in *Texas Rangers* in 2001 with James Van Der Beek. Travis also played in the TV series *Touched by an Angel.*

In 2016, Randy Travis was inducted into the Country Music Hall of Fame. The singer has also won 10 AMA Awards, 9 ACM Awards, 8 Dove Awards, 6 Grammy Awards, and 6 CMA Awards. He also has a star on the Hollywood Walk of Fame.

And to think that it all started out in Marshville, North Carolina!

This American Novelist Was From North Carolina

Did you know that American novelist Thomas Wolfe was from North Carolina?

Referred to as the greatest talent of his generation, the early 20th-century author wrote four novels, along with a number of other works. His books, which were written from the 1920s to the 1940s, give Wolfe's perspective of American culture during the time period.

Tomas Wolfe's first novel, *Look Homeward, Angel*, is known for its strong imagery of Western North Carolina.

Wolfe is widely considered to be one of the most important authors in modern American literature and North Carolina's most famous writer. He was also one of the first to master autobiographical fiction.

Thomas Wolfe was born at 92 Woodfin Street in Asheville, North Carolina. He studied at the University of North Carolina-Chapel Hill when he was just 15 years old. He wrote a play that was performed by students at the school and also worked on the UNC's student newspaper, *The Daily Tar Heel*.

During his time at UNC, Wolfe allegedly made a prediction: his portrait would hang in New West. That's where his portrait can be found today.

RANDOM FACTS

1. Country musician Eric Church is from Granite Falls, North Carolina. He started playing the guitar and writing songs at the age of 13. By his senior year in high school, he had landed a local gig. Church attended South Caldwell High School in Hudson, NC and Appalachian State University in Boone, North Carolina before moving to Nashville. He's gone on to have a number of hit songs, including "Talladega," "Give Me Back My Hometown," "Like a Wrecking Ball," and "Raise Me Up" (featuring Keith Urban).

2. Edward Snowden is from Elizabeth City, North Carolina.

3. Loudon Wainwright III was born in Chapel Hill, North Carolina. The folk singer/songwriter and actor is perhaps most well-known for being father to Rufus Wainwright, Martha Wainwright, and Lucy Wainwright Roche.

4. Star Jones, former co-host of the ABC morning talk show *The View*, was born in Badin, North Carolina.

5. Tori Amos is considered one of the greatest Rock and Roll singers of all time. She was born at Old

Catawba Hospital in Newton, North Carolina when her parents were on a trip away from their home in Washington, D.C.

6. Zach Galifianakis is an actor/comedian, who's most well-known for his roles in *The Hangover*, *Due Date*, *Birdman*, *Masterminds*, and *The Lego Batman Movie*. Galifianakis as born in Wilkesboro, North Carolina and graduated from Wilkes Central High School. Although he attended North Carolina State University, he didn't graduate from it.

7. Evan Rachel Wood is most well-known for her roles as Tracy in the movie *Thirteen* and Dolores in the HBO series *Westworld*. Wood also gained a lot of attention for her previous relationship with Marilyn Manson, who wrote the song "Heart-Shaped Glasses" about her. Wood was born in Raleigh, North Carolina. She attended Cary Elementary in Cary, North Carolina for a short time before being homeschooled.

8. Earl Scruggs and the "Foggy Mountain Boys" helped introduced bluegrass music to pop culture on TV. Scruggs was the first to introduce his three-finger banjo-picking style, which is known as "Scruggs Style," to bluegrass music. Scruggs was from Flint Hill, North Carolina.

9. Actress Jada Pinkett Smith went to North Carolina School of the Arts.

10. Author Sarah Dessen was born in Illinois, but she moved to Chapel Hill, North Carolina at a young age. She graduated from the University of North Carolina-Chapel Hill, where she majored in Creative Writing. Dessen worked at the Flying Burrito restaurant in Chapel Hill, where she waitressed until her first young adult novel, *That Summer*, was published. Her book *Along for the Ride* made the author a NY Times best-selling author.

11. Actress Mary-Louise Parker graduated from the North Carolina School of the Arts. Parker is most well-known for her role as Nancy Botwin, the main character in the show *Weeds*. She also played in *Fried Green Tomatoes*, *Red/Red 2*, and *The Spiderwick Chronicles.*

12. Country singer Chris Lane is from Kernersville, North Carolina. The musician is most well-known for his songs "Take Back Home Girl" (which hit No. 55 on the *Billboard* Hot 100) and "I Don't Know About You."

13. The late Soul/R&B musician Ben E. King was from Henderson, North Carolina. King is most well-known for his songs "Save the Last Dance for Me" and "Stand By Me."

14. Country singer Luke Combs was born in Charlotte and moved to Asheville when he was eight years old. He went to Appalachian State

University in Boone, North Carolina. It was there that he played his first country music show at the Parthenon Café. Today, Combs is known for his hit singles "Hurricane," "She Got the Best of Me," and "One Number Away."

15. Musician Ryan Adams is from Raleigh, North Carolina. Adams is Mandy Moore's ex-husband.

16. Humorist David Sedaris, who writes for *The New Yorker*, grew up near Raleigh, North Carolina.

17. Fred Durst, formerly of the band Limp Bizkit, was born in Gastonia, North Carolina. He lived there until he was two years old.

18. Actress Chyler Leigh West was born in Charlotte, North Carolina. She's most recognized for her roles as Lexie Grey in *Grey's Anatomy* and Janey in the movie *Not Another Teen Movie.*

19. Chelsea Cooley is from Charlotte, North Carolina. She won the Miss North Carolina Teen USA in 2000. She later placed second runner-up in the Miss USA 2004 pageant and won Miss North Carolina in 2005 her second time trying. She also competed in the Miss Universe pageant in 2005, in which she placed in the top 10.

20. Actor John Newton was born in Chapel Hill, North Carolina. He's best-known for his roles as Clark Kent in the show *Superboy* and Ryan McBride in the show *Melrose Place.*

Test Yourself – Questions

1. Which of the following *American Idol* contestants was <u>not</u> from North Carolina?

   a. Carrie Underwood
   b. Kellie Pickler
   c. Fantasia Barrino

2. Andy Griffith's hometown was:

   a. Asheville, North Carolina
   b. Mount Airy, North Carolina
   c. Boone, North Carolina

3. The only Nicholas Sparks movie that was <u>not</u> set primarily in North Carolina was:

   a. *A Walk to Remember*
   b. *The Longest Ride*
   c. *The Last Song*

4. Which iconic Hollywood actress was from North Carolina?

   a. Marilyn Monroe
   b. Audrey Hepburn
   c. Ava Gardner

5. Which town is known to be the heart of North Carolina's film industry?

   a. Charlotte
   b. Wilmington
   c. Raleigh

Answers

1. a.
2. b.
3. c.
4. c.
5. b.

CHAPTER THREE

NORTH CAROLINA'S INVENTIONS, IDEAS, AND MORE

Have you ever wondered what inventions have come out of North Carolina? A number of famous products and businesses have started out in the Tar Heel State. Did you know which fast food chains have come out of the state? Do you know which famous soda was invented in the state? Do you know which home improvements store got started out in the state or which modern merchandise technology that's used worldwide started out in Raleigh, North Carolina? Do you know which pickle company was established in the state? To find out more about North Carolina's inventions, ideas, and more, read on!

Krispy Kreme Doughnuts

Did you know that Krispy Kreme Doughnuts got their start in Winston-Salem?

Krispy Kreme Doughnut founder Vernon Rudolph purchased a yeast-based donuts recipe from a chef in New Orleans.

In 1937, Vernon moved to open a doughnut shop in Winston-Salem, North Carolina. Rumor has it that he chose that location because Camel Cigarettes, his favorite cigarette company, was also headquartered there.

Vernon sold the majority of his Krispy Kreme doughnuts to convenience stores. Between midnight and 4 a.m., he also sold doughnuts to customers who came into the shop while they were being produced.

The first Krispy Kreme Doughnuts store was located in a rented building on South Main Street in present-day historic Old Salem.

From there, Vernon began to expand his business. By the 1960s, Krispy Kreme was popular throughout the Southeastern U.S.

In 2001, Krispy Kreme's first international location opened in Ontario, Canada.

As of 2015, Krispy Kreme had 1,000 stores.

The company's headquarters have remained in Winston-Salem to this day.

Every year in Raleigh, North Carolina, the company is celebrated when 8,000 people compete in the Krispy Kreme Challenge. Contestants try to eat 12 doughnuts while they run 5 miles in just one hour's time. The challenge is done to raise money for a children's hospital in Raleigh.

"Putt-Putt" Miniature Golf and the First Miniature Golf Course

Today, it's a favorite American pastime. But did you know that "Putt-Putt" miniature golf was invented in the Tar Heel State? Or that the state was home to the first miniature golf course in the United States?

Putt-Putt golf was invented in Fayetteville, North Carolina. In 1954, a businessman named Don Clayton opened the first course.

What sets Putt-Putt apart from miniature golf? It focused more on one's putting abilities than the windmills and scenery often associated with miniature golf courses.

Since Clayton opened his first course in Fayetteville, his company has gone on to build 200 more Putt-Putt courses across the country.

Additionally, the first *ever* miniature golf course in the country can also be found in North Carolina. An Englishman names James Wells Barber had the first miniature golf course constructed on his estate in Pinehurst, North Carolina back in 1919. The course was named "Thistle Dhu" (allegedly because the builders of the course said, "This'll do"). The 18-hole golf course was originally intended for experienced golfers, not children.

Pinehurst Resort now offers a Thistle Dhu miniature golf course that's designed to resemble the original course.

State Art Museums

Today, state art museums are a favorite pastime for many. But did you know that North Carolina was the first U.S. state to introduce state art museums?

The North Carolina Museum of Art opened in Raleigh back in 1956. It was the first major museum to be established due to state legislation and funding.

Today, the museum is home to over 40 galleries, more than a dozen major works of art, an outdoor amphitheater, and a 164-acre park. It's one of the leading art museums in the Southern U.S. and paved the way to other state-funded art museums across the country.

Pepsi

Pepsi is one of the most popular soft drinks of all-time. Did you know that it was invented in North Carolina during the late 1800s?

The soft drink was invented by a drugstore employee named Caleb Bradham back in 1893. He sold it at the soda fountain in the drugstore he worked at in New Bern, North Carolina.

Caleb Bradham, who was training to be a doctor at the time, believed that Pepsi helped with digestion. His drink was originally called "Brad's Drink," but he renamed it "Pepsi-Cola" in 1898. The name came from the word "dyspepsia," meaning indigestion. (The drink wouldn't become known as simply "Pepsi" until 1961).

Bradham also thought the drink could help boost energy.

By 1902, there was so much demand for Bradham's soft drink that he filed incorporation papers with the state of North Carolina to established corporate branches in Pennsylvania, New York, Maryland, and Virginia.

Today, you can still visit the place where Pepsi-Cola was invented in New Bern. There, you can enjoy fountain Pepsi and check out classic bottles, vintage signage, and more.

Cheerwine

If you've never heard of Cheerwine, you've probably never been to North Carolina. The wild-cherry flavored soda is very popular in the state, so it may come as no surprise that it was also invented there.

Cheerwine is known for its mildly sweet flavor, which has strong black cherry notes. The soda is burgundy in color. It also has a higher level of carbonation in comparison to other sodas. The drink was named for its color and flavor. Despite the "wine" in the drink's name, it's not actually a wine and doesn't contain any alcohol.

The idea for Cheerwine came about when L.D. Peeler wanted to invent a new, unique soft drink. He purchased flavors from a traveling salesman and designed the drink in the basement of his wholesale grocery store in Salisbury, North Carolina. He designed the drink during a sugar shortage that happened during World War I.

A few years after he created Cheerwine, Peeler's fizzy drink hit the market and saw much success. It has even earned the nickname of the "nectar of the tar heels."

Today, the drink can be found throughout the South and California.

The annual Cheerwine Festival takes place in downtown Salisbury every year in May. In addition to live music, you'll also find North Carolina pulled pork in Cheerwine BBQ sauce, Cheerwine merchandise, and, last but certainly not least, Cheerwine.

Vicks VapoRub

Vicks VapoRub can be a lifesaver when you're suffering from a bad cough or chest congestion. Some even use it for joint and muscle aches. Did you know that Vicks VapoRub got its start in North Carolina?

Vicks VapoRub was developed by a Selma, North Carolina pharmacist named Lunsford Richardson. The drugstore sold Ben-Gay and Richardson had heard his customers mention that it helped provide sinus relief. Richardson blended menthol into petroleum jelly. He called it Richardson's Croup and Pneumonia Cure Salve before eventually naming it Vicks VapoRub. The ointment was named after Richardson's brother-in-law, Josh Vick. Vick was a physician who provided Richardson access to a laboratory from which he created the product.

When Richardson began selling the ointment back in 1905, it was through his company, which he called Richardson-Vicks, Inc. The company was based in Greensboro, North Carolina. Procter & Gamble bought the company out in 1985. Today, the company is now known as Vicks.

Now, it's a common household name and it all started out in Selma, NC!

The Barcode

Today, the barcode is used throughout the entire world. It forever changed the way we can track merchandise and can purchase items simply by scanning a code. But have you ever thought about how it came to be? Did you know that the barcode started out in Raleigh, North Carolina?

George Lauer was given the task of making a universal supermarket scanner and label. He presented his proposal for the scanner in 1972 in front of the Super Marker Committee in Rochester, New York, who (obviously) liked his idea.

Lowe's

Lowe's is a home improvement store with more than 2,300 locations throughout North America. It's the 2nd leading hardware chain, surpassed only by The Home Depot. Did you know that Lowe's started out in Wilkesboro, North Carolina?

Lowe's was started by Lucius Smith Lowe in 1921. When Lowe's first started out, it sold an array of products, including groceries, produce, dry goods, and more.

After Lowe's death in 1940, his daughter Ruth inherited the business. She sold it to her brother Jim, who added Carl Buchan as a partner in 1943. Buchan believed that there was going to be a dramatic increased in production following World War II, which is when the store shifted to selling hardware and building materials.

The second Lowe's store opened in Sparta, North Carolina in 1949, 28 years after the first location had opened.

In 1952, Buchan and Lowe had differences in opinion when it came to expansion of the company. The two had other joint ventures together. When they split, Lowe took control of the other businesses and Buchan became the sole owner of Lowe's.

Buchan began to expand the company by opening many other stores throughout North Carolina, including in Charlotte, Asheville, and Durham.

After Buchan died of a heart attack in 1961, the executive team took the company public. By the following years, there were 21 Lowe's locations and annual revenues of $32 million.

During the 1980s, Lowe's suffered due to competition with The Home Depot.

Since then, Lowe's has grown throughout the United States. Although its locations were found through the U.S.A., Canada, and Mexico, the company announced in 2018 that it would close its Mexico locations.

Texas Pete Hot Sauce

Don't let the name fool you—Texas Pete Hot Sauce was *not* invented in Texas. It was actually created by Thad Garner whose father Sam Garner owned the Dixie Pig Barbeque Stand in Winston-Salem back in 1929. They developed the hot sauce to offer his customers something spicier. They originally made the hot sauce from a stove in their home.

So, where did the word "Texas" in the hot sauce's

name come from? A marketing adviser originally recommended that the hot sauce be called "Mexican Joe" due to the spiciness factor of Mexican food. Thad Garner's father insisted that he keep the name American, however. Texas was known for its spicy food and the name "Pete" was chosen because it was Thad's brother Harold's nickname.

As of 2004, Texas Pete Hot Sauce is the 3rd best-selling hot sauce brand in America.

Texas Pete is celebrated each year at the Texas Pete Spirits of Summer festival, which happens in Winston-Salem. There's live music, food, and regional alcoholic beverages.

The Mt. Olive Pickle Company

Today, it's the top-selling pickle brand in the southeastern United States and the largest independent pickle company in America. But did you know that the Mt. Olive Pickle Company started out in—you guessed it—Mt. Olive, North Carolina.

During the mid-1920s, a Lebanese immigrant named Shikrey Baddour noticed how much cucumber crop ended up being wasted by farmers in the Goldsboro, North Carolina area (near Mt. Olive).

Baddour had the idea of buying the cucumbers, brining them, and then selling them to other pickle farms. He went into business with George Moore, who was a sailor from Wilmington who had worked in a pickle plant.

When their plan turned out to be unsuccessful and they didn't have buyers for their pickles, they came up with a new plan. In 1926, they established Mt. Olive Pickle Company, Inc., under the lead of a businessman named Headley Morris Cox, who became President of the company.

Today, Mt. Olive is the largest privately held pickle company in the United States. Back in 1926, there were originally 37 shareholders who invested $19,000 in capital to get the company going. They viewed the company as something that would benefit the community. Today, most of the stockholders are grandchildren and great-grandchildren of the original 37 investors.

When the company first opened in 1926, the building it operated out of was just 3,600 square feet. In 2005, the plant expanded to 970,000 square feet.

The Mt. Olive Pickle Company is celebrated in a couple of ways throughout the state. For starters, there's a North Carolina Pickle Festival that's held annually, which Mt. Olive Pickle co-founded back in 1986.

There's also a New Year's Eve Pickle Drop that happens in Mt. Olive every year. On December 31st at 7 p.m., a 3-foot pickle is lowered down a 45-foot flagpole into a pickle tank.

Bojangles

Bojangles is known for its fried chicken, mac and cheese, Bo-Berry biscuits, and sweet tea. Did you know that the first Bojangles restaurant opened in Charlotte, North Carolina back in 1977?

Jack Fulk and Richard Thomas founded the fast food chain. The concept of the restaurant was based on three attributes: 1). Distinct flavor 2). Homemade products made from scratch, and 3). Friendly service in a festively designed restaurant.

Today, there are over 600 Bojangles locations throughout the United States.

If you happen to visit a North Carolina Panthers home game in Charlotte, you may find "Bo Time" food boxes, which are large boxes packed with food from Bojangles.

Hardee's

Hardee's is a popular fast food chain located primarily throughout America's South and Midwest. The restaurant is famous for its curly fries. Did you know the chain got its start in North Carolina?

Wilber Hardee opened the first Hardee's restaurant in Greenville, North Carolina in 1960. When the restaurant proved to be successful during its first year, Hardee's expanded and opened its first company store in Rock Mount, North Carolina, with the help of James Carson Gardner and Leonard

Rawls. (Later, Hardee said that Gardner and Rawls won a controlling share of the company from him during a poker game. Hardee later sold the rest of his shares to them).

Gardner and Rawls sold the original Hardee's franchises to friends and acquaintances.

By the early 1970s, Hardee's had opened 200 stores, as well as its first international location in Germany.

In 1997, Hardee's merged with Carl Jr.'s.

To date, there are more than 3,100 Hardee's restaurants in 40 states and 10 foreign countries.

Lance Crackers

You might not recognize the name, but you've probably tried Lance crackers at some point. They're those orange crackers that are filled with peanut butter. Did you know they originated from Charlotte, North Carolina?

Back in 1913, a food broker named Phillip Lance found himself stuck with 500 pounds of peanuts. He had the idea to roast and sell the nuts for $5 a bag. The nuts were an instant success, leading Lance to expand his line to peanut butter.

In 1915, Lance's wife Mary and their two daughters started spreading the peanut butter between two crackers, leading to the birth of the peanut butter cracker sandwich.

Golden Corral

Did you know that one of America's favorite "all you can eat" buffets was started out in North Carolina?

Back in 1973, James Maynard and William F. Carl Gavone Siamese opened the first Golden Corral in Fayetteville, North Carolina.

Although Golden Corral is most well-known for its buffet, the restaurants also offer a grill, carving station, and the Brass Bell Bakery.

As of 2017, there were 487 locations. The restaurant can be found in 48 U.S. states and Puerto Rico.

Food Lion

Food Lion is one of the most well-known grocery stores in the South, but did you know that it started out in North Carolina?

Food Lion was originally opened as Food Town in Salisbury, North Carolina back in 1957 by cofounders Wilson Smith, Ralph Ketner, and Brown Ketner. In 1974, Food Town was acquired by a Belgium-based grocery company.

The name was changed to Food Town when expansion took place in Virginia. There were already a few grocery stores called Foodtown, so the name Food Lion came about in 1983.

RANDOM FACTS

1. The Ctrl+Alt+Del computer function was invented by an IBM worker named David Bradley. Bradley worked in the Research Triangle Park. The function is used to terminate an application task or have the computer restart itself.

2. Three headache powder brands were all invented in North Carolina. The most well-known headache powder is Goody's Headache Powder, which was invented in Winston-Salem in 1932. BC Headache Powder was invented before that in 1906 in Durham, followed by Stanback Headache Powder in Salisbury, North Carolina in 1911. Headache powders are designed to be faster-acting than capsules or pills.

3. The Fresh Market was started back in 1982 in Greensboro, North Carolina, where its headquarters remain to this day. The Fresh Market is a specialty store known for its high-end groceries. There are 100 stories in 18 states across the country.

4. Ingles grocery store was founded by Robert P. Ingle, who opened the first store in Asheville, North Carolina. The store now has approximately 200 locations in six states in the Southeast.

5. Harris Teeter was started by the merging of two grocery stores. Harris Super Markets was started by W.T. Harris back in 1936 in Charlotte, North Carolina. He opened the first location on $500, which he borrowed. In 1939, brothers Paul and Willis L. Teeter started Teeter's Food Mart, which they opened in Mooresville, NC. In 1960, Harris Super Markets and Teeter's Food Marts merged with what we know today as Harris Teeter Super Markets, Inc.

6. Earth Fare was born in 1975 when Roger Derrough started the first natural foods store in Asheville, North Carolina. The store operated in a tiny storefront before eventually relocating to Broadway Avenue in Asheville.

7. Carolina Treet BBQ Sauce and Bone Suckin' Sauce were developed in Wilmington. Back in 1953, the sauce was developed in the meat cutting room of an independent grocery store. It was originally intended to barbecue whole pre-prepared chickens. Soon, people started asking if they could have more of the BBQ sauce to use at home. Today, Carolina Treet's sauces can be found at grocery stores throughout the entire country.

8. Neese's Sausage was founded in Greensboro North Carolina in 1933. J.T. Neese's special recipe was first sold back in 1917 via a covered wagon.

9. Bertie County Peanuts was started in Windsor in 1915. The peanuts, which were originally roasted in a popcorn popper by founder "Papa Jack" Powell Sr., are now sold across the country.

10. Lowes Foods is a regional supermarket chain that was started by Alex Lee in Winston-Salem back in 1954. It was later bought by Carl Buchan, who previously owned Lowe's home improvement stores. There are more than 100 locations throughout North Carolina, South Carolina, and Virginia.

11. Lone Star Steakhouse & Saloon is a restaurant chain that was first started in Winston-Salem, North Carolina in 1989. By the 1990s, there were 265 Lone Star restaurants.

12. Cook Out is a fast food restaurant chain with 244 locations in 10 U.S. states. The first Cook Out restaurant was opened in Greensboro, North Carolina by Morris Reaves back in 1989. The restaurant is known for its famous North Carolina barbecue, in addition to hamburgers, hot dogs, and chicken sandwiches.

13. Family Dollar opened its first store in Charlotte, North Carolina in 1959. It was founded by a 21-year-old named Leon Levine. The following year, the first South Carolina location opened. By 1969, there were 50 stores in Charlotte alone. Today,

Family Dollar is now owned by Dollar Tree and there are more than 8,000 Family Dollar locations through the United States.

14. Although Levi Strauss & Jacob Davis were the first to begin mass producing overalls for the public in the 1890s, they were actually invented by Abigail Carter of Clinton, North Carolina who, in 1859, invented overalls for her railroad engineer husband.

15. Adam & Eve is the leading mail-order distributor of condoms, sex toys, and erotica in America. The company was founded by physicians Tim Black and Phil Harvey in Chapel Hill, back in 1970. Before it offered a catalog, Adam & Eve was originally started as a small store in Chapel Hill where it sold condoms and lubricants.

16. While barbecue didn't originate from North Carolina, the state does have a unique cooking method when it comes to pulled pork. In the Tar Heel State, there are two main ways to make pulled pork: 1. Smoke the whole pig and serve it with a vinegar-based sauce or 2). Smoke the shoulder style and serve it with a tomato-based sauce.

17. Wicked Weed Brewery is one of the most popular breweries in Asheville, North Carolina, which is known for its craft beer. The brewery is known for its sour beers.

18. The first bobbin-less sewing machine was invented in 1940 by Beulah Louise Henry. Henry, who had been nicknamed "Lady Edison," was a popular inventor from Charlotte, North Carolina.

19. Beulah Louise Henry also invented "Miss Illusion," a doll with eyes that could open, close, and change color, in 1935.

20. The "protograph," which was a typewriter accessory that could make copies of documents, was another one of Lady Edison's inventions.

Test Yourself – Questions

1. Which grocery store was <u>not</u> founded in North Carolina?

    a. Food Lion
    b. Kroger
    c. Ingles

2. Pepsi was originally called:

    a. Chad's Drink
    b. Caleb's Drink
    c. Brad's Drink

3. The first "putt-putt" miniature golf course was built in:

    a. Raleigh, North Carolina
    b. Fayetteville, North Carolina
    c. Asheville, North Carolina

4. Which fast food chain was <u>not</u> started in North Carolina?

    a. Hardee's
    b. Bojangles
    c. In-N-Out Burger

5. Which popular clothing item was invented in North Carolina?

    a. Overalls
    b. Leggings
    c. Jumpsuits

Answers

1. b.

2. c.

3. b.

4. c.

5. a.

CHAPTER FOUR

NORTH CAROLINA'S ATTRACTIONS

If you're planning a trip to North Carolina, you might be wondering what attractions the state has to offer. Do you know about the most famous home in the Tar Heel State? Do you know about the record-breaking waterfall in the state? What about North Carolina's most famous battleship or its most significant mountain? Do you know about the museum that's dedicated to the life and death of North Carolina's most famous pirate? Read on to learn more about these and other North Carolina's attractions.

The Largest Home in America is in North Carolina

Did you know that the largest home in the *entire country* is located in the Tar Heel State?

Located in Asheville, North Carolina, the Biltmore

State is a private estate that encompasses 178,926 square feet. There are 256 rooms and an enormous garden that can be found at the estate.

The home was built for George Washington Vanderbilt II, who was the youngest son of William Henry Vanderbilt of the prominent Vanderbilt family. It was built during the Gilded Age and is considered to be one of the most significant examples of architecture during this time period.

Construction of the estate started in 1889 and lasted six years, ending in 1896. It was such a large construction project that 32,000 bricks were built in a brick kiln on the construction site. A three-mile railroad spur was also built to get materials to the construction site more easily. More than 1000 workers and 60 stonemasons were needed for the project.

As for the home's furnishings, Vanderbilt went on trips overseas where he bought carpets, linens, and various other types of décor. Some of the American-bought items included a grand piano, rocking chairs, and an oak drop-front desk.

George Washington Vanderbilt II named the estate himself. "Bilt" originated from "Bildt," which was where the Vanderbilt family originally came from in Holland. He chose "more" due to the Anglo-Saxon word meaning "open, rolling land."

Vanderbilt first invited friends and family to his estate on Christmas Eve of 1895. In the years that followed, the estate saw a number of notable guests, including presidents, ambassadors, and authors Edith Wharton and Henry James.

To this day, the home is owned by George Vanderbilt's descendants.

Today, the Biltmore Estate is open to tourists. It sees approximately 1.4 million visitors a year. It's recommended that tourists allow themselves at least one—if not two—days to tour the estate, gardens, and the famous Biltmore Winery.

Pisgah National Forest Was Established Thanks to Biltmore Estate

Today, the Pisgah National Forest spans across 512,758 acres in the Appalachian Mountains. It includes parts of both the Blue Ridge Mountains and the Great Balsam Mountains.

As of 2017, the Pisgah National Forest saw 4.6 million visitors a year.

But do you know how the national forest got started in the first place?

After George Washington Vanderbilt II died in 1914, his widow, Edith, sold some of the property from the Biltmore Estate. The decision to sell was to honor Vanderbilt's wishes to create the core of the Pisgah

National Forest. The United States Forest Service purchased over 86,000 acres from the widow. They paid $5 an acre.

Two years later, in 1916, the Pisgah National Forest was established. It was one of the first national forests to ever have been founded in Eastern America.

This Record-Breaking Mountain is Located in North Carolina

Did you know that North Carolina is home to one of the most significant mountains in the entire country?

Mount Mitchell is not only the highest point in the Appalachians, but it's also the highest point in the entire Eastern United States. With its highest elevation of 6,684 feet above sea level, Mount Mitchell is the highest mountain located east of the Mississippi River.

Mount Mitchell is located in Burnsville, North Carolina. The mountain is located in Mount Mitchell State Park, which is surrounded by the Pisgah National Forest.

The mountain was originally called Black Dome due to its round shape. However, it was later named after a professor at the University of North Carolina named Elisha Mitchell, who explored the area in 1835. Elisha Mitchell was the first to determine that the mountain was at a higher elevation than Mount Washington in New Hampshire, which was previously believed to be the highest point east of the Rocky Mountains. When Mitchell returned to the area to verify his first measurements in 1857, he fell and died at Mitchell Falls.

As of 2015, Mount Mitchell State Park saw approximately 315,979 visitors a year.

North Carolina is Home to This Famous Lighthouse

Did you know that North Carolina is home to one of the most significant lighthouses in the entire world?

Cape Hatteras Light, which is located on Hatteras Island in the Outer Banks, is one of the most famous lighthouses in the world. This is because, at 210 feet high, it's the tallest brick lighthouse structure in America and the second tallest in the entire world! (The No. 1 tallest brick lighthouse in the world is Świnoujście Lighthouse in Poland, which stands at 213 feet tall).

You might remember from Chapter One that the Outer Banks was home to a number of shipwrecks, leading to its nickname of the "Graveyard of the Atlantic."

As a result, Congress appropriated $44,000 for Cape Hatteras Lighthouse in 1794. The lighthouse was built in 1802.

The lighthouse's light marked dangerous shoals that extended to the cape. The lighthouse that stands today isn't the original lighthouse. The original tower was built of dark sandstone and its light consisted of 18 lamps. The new and improved lighthouse, which was built in 1868 and completed in 1870, improved the light and was made of brick. When it was first built, the Cape Hatteras Light the tallest brick lighthouse in the world.

Despite being the tallest brick lighthouse in the world, it only has the 15 the highest light in the United States. The other 14 lighthouses that surpass it are built at higher elevations.

The Blue Ridge Parkway is One of the Most Scenic Parkways in the USA

The Blue Ridge Parkway is known to be one of the most scenic parkways in all of America. Chances are, you may have seen the picturesque parkway on calendars, postcards, and more!

The parkway, which spans across 469 miles, is the longest linear park in the country. It runs through 29 counties in both North Carolina and Virginia. The parkway links the Great Smoky Mountains National Park and the Shenandoah National Park, with the bulk of its scenery being along the Blue Ridge Mountains.

The Blue Ridge Parkway was built back in 1935. At the time, it was originally known as the Appalachian Scenic Highway. Its name was changed to the Blue Ridge Parkway in 1936.

With more than 15 million annual visitors, the Blue Ridge Parkway has been the most visited unit of the National Park System nearly every year. The land surrounding the road is owned and maintained by the National Park Service.

You Can Visit the Blackbeard Museum in the Outer Banks

Blackbeard's legacy is one of the biggest draws for tourists on Ocracoke Island in the Outer Banks. Did you know that you can visit a museum that honors the famous pirate?

There's an inlet on Ocracoke Island known as "Teach's Hole," which was named in honor of Blackbeard. Today, it operates as both a Blackbeard museum and a pirate specialty shop. You'll find a 2-part documentary on Blackbeard's life and death. The museum is also home to the largest collection of pirate paraphernalia on the Outer Banks. Some of the things you'll find on exhibit include pirate weapons, flags, swords, maps, old bottles, books, music, a life-sized figure of Blackbeard, and more. You'll also find pirate flags, party supplies, and more for sale at the specialty shop.

You Can See Shipwrecks at the Graveyard of the Atlantic Museum

With the Outer Banks' nickname of the "Graveyard of the Atlantic," it may not come as a surprise that there's a museum to honor the many shipwrecks that have happened in the area. The Graveyard of the Atlantic Museum operates all year long and features exhibits and artifacts that preserve the region's maritime culture.

The exhibits include artifacts found from shipwrecks, ship models, explorers, colonists, pirates, and maritime military displays from the American Civil War and World War II. In the lobby, you'll find the original First Order Lens from the Cape Hatteras Lighthouse, which dates back to 1854. There's also a gift shop on the site of the museum.

The Most Visited National Park is in North Carolina

Did you know that the most visited national park in the entire United States is located in North Carolina?

Great Smoky Mountains National Park draws in more than 10 million visitors a year. This is double the number of visitors the second most visited U.S. national park—Grand Canyon National Park—sees annually. Since the park was established in 1931, over a half a billion people have visited the park.

Great Smoky Mountains National Park, which runs through both North Carolina and Tennessee, is rich in history. It was once home to the Cherokee Indian tribe.

Today, the park is known for its mountains—which are some of the oldest mountains in the world—and its wildlife. The park is also home to about 1,500 species of wildflowers. Some of the animals you can expect to see within the park include black bear, white-tailed deer, coyote, red and gray fox, red wolf, wild boar, river otter, wild turkey, and elk. The park is also known as the "Salamander Capital of the World." It earned this nickname because it's home to about 30 species of salamanders!

Clingman's Dome is one of the most popular spots in the park. At 6,643 feet, it's the highest point in Great Smoky Mountains National Park. It's also the 2nd highest point east of the Mississippi (surpassed only by Mount Mitchell).

Cherokee, North Carolina is the main entrance from the North Carolina side of the park.

The Wright Brothers National Memorial Honors the Aviator Brothers

Knowing that Wilbur and Orville Wright made their first flight in North Carolina, it probably won't surprise you to know that the Wright Brothers National Memorial can be found in the state, too.

Located in Kitty Hawk, North Carolina, the site commemorates the area where the Wright Brothers had their first successful flight in a heavier-than-air prototype. The brothers chose the site due to the steady winds and seclusion of the area. Back in 1903, the Wrights made four flights from the ground near the base of the hill at the Kitty Hawk national memorial site and conducted many gliding experiments on the shifting dune during the next three years. The dune is what is now known as Kill Devil Hill.

Today, you can walk the routes of the Wright Brothers' four flights. There's also a Visitor Center, which is home to a museum that features models, tools, and machines that were used by the famous aviator brothers. There's a life-size replica of the 1903 flyer the Wright Brothers used, which was the first heavier-than-air aircraft in history to ever be successfully flown. There's also a full-scale model of the 1902 glider, which was constructed under Orville Wright's instruction. The museum also features portraits and photographs of other famous aviation pioneers.

There's also a 60-foot granite monument that honors the achievements of Wilbur and Orville Wright on the site.

The USS *North Carolina* is a Museum with a Historic Past

The USS *North Carolina* has a historic past. It was the first of 10 battleships to enter service during World War II. The U.S. Navy ship destroyed (at minimum) 24 enemy aircraft, sank an enemy troopship and carried out nine shore bombardments over the course of the 300,000 miles it steamed. Ten men died aboard the ship, with many more injured.

Today, the USS *North Carolina* is docked at the Wilmington, North Carolina seaport and serves as a museum ship. When you visit Battleship North Carolina, you can walk her decks, tour the sailor's and officer's quarters, take behind-the-scenes tours, witness reenactments, and more!

The North Carolina Transportation Museum is Huge

Located in Spencer, North Carolina, the N.C. Transportation Museum is known for its 60 acres it encompasses and it's 90,000 square foot Back Shop. To put this into perspective for you, the museum is the size of two football fields. In other words, it's huge!

The museum's exhibits feature rail equipment, steam locomotives, rail equipment, antique automobiles, classic cars and trucks, and more. Perhaps one of the most famous exhibits is the aviation exhibit, which features a full-size replica Wright Flyer. The replica has been loaned to the museum long-term from the Wright Brothers National Memorial.

North Carolina is Home to the "Grand Canyon of the East"

Linville Gorge, which has been nicknamed the "Grand Canyon of the East," is one of the deepest gorges in the Eastern United States.

With its location in the Pisgah National Forest, the Linville River enters the gorge at Linville Falls. There, it drops 90 feet and then spans across 12 miles, surrounded by steep rock walls.

The trails can be easily accessed on the Blue Ridge Parkway. There are four overlooks over the course of a 1.6-mile round-trip hike.

It's something you won't want to miss out on the next time you're in North Carolina!

The Museum of the Cherokee Indian Offers a Unique Cultural Experience

If you're looking to learn more about the Cherokee Indians, you won't want to miss out on the Museum of the Cherokee Indian.

Located in Cherokee, North Carolina, the museum offers exhibits and artifacts that help visitors learn more about the culture, mythology, and history of the Native American tribe. You'll learn more about the British colonists' involvement with the Cherokee Indians of North Carolina. There's also a small movie theater, which offers a short film to help you learn more about the history of the Cherokees.

Visitors will also want to check out the gift shop, which features handmade Cherokee items. You'll find everything from handmade bowls and wooden carvings to baskets and prints. The gift shop is also known for its book section.

The North Carolina Museum of Natural Sciences is Home to This Unique Dinosaur Exhibit

If you're a dinosaur lover, then you won't want to miss out on the North Carolina Museum of Natural Sciences. The museum is home to the only genuine Acrocanthosaurus exhibit *in the entire world*. The skeleton is a part of the "Terror of the South" exhibit. The museum is also known for its "Prehistoric North Carolina" exhibit, which features other prehistoric life throughout both North Carolina and the Southeastern U.S.

The museum is also known for its "Investigating Right Whales" exhibit where you can touch the skeleton of "Slumpy". Slumpy was a North Atlantic Right Whale with a historic past. The whale's death led to the establishment of laws that now require cargo ships to drive at slower speeds in whale migration areas.

The North Carolina Museum of Natural Sciences is the most visited museum in the state as of 2013, drawing in approximately 1.2 million visitors a year. It's also the largest museum of natural sciences in the Southeastern U.S. and the oldest museum in North Carolina.

The North Carolina Zoo Holds Several Records

With its location in Asheboro, the North Carolina Zoo opened in 1974. It sees more than 700,000 visitors each year, and for good reason. The zoo is home to more than 1,600 animals, which includes species from Africa and North America.

Did you know that the North Carolina Zoo has the largest walk-through, natural zoo habitat? In fact, the North Carolina Zoo was actually the first zoo in the United States to try out a "natural habitat" for its animals. Animals are kept on land ranges, which was done in an attempt at reducing behavioral problems that can stem from being kept in close confinement. The African Plains exhibit spans across 37 acres, which is larger than most of the zoos in the country.

In addition, the North Carolina Zoo is also home to the largest number of both chimpanzees and Alaskan seabirds in the United States.

RANDOM FACTS

1. White Lake, which is located near Elizabethtown, is commonly referred to as the country's "safest beach." This is because there are no tides that pose a risk to swimmers. The bottom of the lake is sandy and the water is clear.

2. Grandfather Mountain is another one of North Carolina's most famous mountains. Reaching 5,946 feet, it's the highest peak of the eastern Blue Ridge Mountains

3. Flat Rock, which has earned the nickname of "Little Charleston of the Mountains," is home to shops, art galleries, and restaurants. It's also home to the Flat Rock Playhouse, which puts on a variety of live shows and musicals. St. John in the Wilderness Episcopal Church is a popular spot for tourists. The church, which dates back to 1833, features an original organ.

4. Linville Caverns are privately-owned, active limestone caverns that are open to the public. The caverns are located just south of Linville Falls in McDowell County.

5. Upper Whitewater Falls in Whitewater River, North Carolina is one of the tallest waterfalls east

of the Mississippi. Some say that it's *the* tallest, but it's argued that Crabtree Falls in Virginia is the actual tallest.

6. Marbles Kids Museum is an interactive, play-based museum for kids located in Raleigh, North Carolina. The museum's stainless-steel wall grid inset contains 1.2 million marbles!

7. Hanging Rock State Park, which is located near Winston-Salem, provides 18 miles of trails for hiking. It also has a lake and is a popular camping spot in the state.

8. Discovery Place is a science and technology museum. Located in Charlotte, NC, Discovery Place is also home to the largest IMAX Dome Theater in the Carolinas.

9. Fort Fisher State Historic Site was a Confederate fort during the American Civil War. Located on Cape Fear, the main fort complex, museum, and visitor center are open to tourists.

10. Fort Macon State Park is the 2nd most visited state park in North Carolina. Located on Bogue Banks, the park draws in 1.3 million visitors a year. The Battle of Fort Macon was fought on the site.

11. Located in Charlotte, Carowinds is a 389-acre amusement park that offers rides on a boardwalk. It's also home to a number of thrill rides, a water

park, wave pool, Peanuts-inspired rides for kids, and more!

12. The North Carolina Aquarium has four locations: Roanoke Island, Fort Fisher, Pine Knoll Shores, and Jennette's Pier. Although Jenette's Pier isn't an actual aquarium, you can see marine animals—including humpback whales—in their natural habitat.

13. Chimney Rock State Park, which is near Asheville, NC, is famous for its 300-foot monolith that the park is named after. To reach to the top of the Chimney Rock, you can either climb 500 steps or take a 26-story elevator.

14. Bald Head Island is an island that you can get to by taking a ferry off the coast of Southport, NC. The island offers 14 miles of beaches, a laidback atmosphere, maritime forests, the Bald Head Island Golf Course, and Turtle Walks during the summer months when sea turtles give birth on the island!

15. Old Salem provides visitors with an insight into what life was like in Winston-Salem during the 18th and 19th centuries. You'll find reenactments and can watch tailors, blacksmiths, shoemakers, and others perform their trades.

16. The U.S. National Whitewater Center in Charlotte is the largest man-made whitewater park in the

country. You can go whitewater rafting, canoeing, kayaking, rock climbing, ziplining, repelling, and more at the park. A number of festivals also take place at the park each year.

17. The Asheville Pinball Museum features 35 pinball machines that visitors can play at one price.

18. Tweetsie Railroad, which is located in Blowing Rock, NC, is a Wild West family theme park. It has amusement rides, live shows, a zoo, and a number of other attractions.

19. Woods of Terror, which is located near Greensboro, is a haunted theme park.

20. Harrah's Cherokee Casino Resort is a hotel and casino located in Cherokee, North Carolina on the Cherokee Indian Reserve. The hotel and casino, along with its sister casino (Harrah's Cherokee Valley River Casino in Murphy, NC), is owned by the Eastern Band of Cherokee Indians.

Test Yourself – Questions

1. The Great Smoky Mountains National Park is the:

   a. Largest national park
   b. Smallest national park
   c. Most visited national park

2. How many rooms can be found in the Biltmore Estate?

   a. 250
   b. 256
   c. 252

3. The most visited museum in North Carolina is:

   a. The Museum of the Cherokee Indian
   b. The North Carolina Museum of Natural Sciences
   c. The Asheville Pinball Museum

4. The Blackbeard Museum can be found at:

   a. Teach's Hole
   b. Pirate's Hole
   c. Teach's Cave

5. Which of North Carolina's beaches has been called the safest beach in the country?

   a. White Lake
   b. Bald Head Island
   c. Hatteras Island

Answers

1. c.
2. b.
3. b.
4. a.
5. a.

CHAPTER FIVE

NORTH CAROLINA'S SPORTS

North Carolina is a state that's rich in sports history. Do you know which MLB player hit his first home run (and gained his infamous nickname) in the state? Do you know which NBA legend grew up in the Tar Heel State? How much do you know about North Carolina's sports teams? Do you know what the official state sport is? Hint: It's the same sport that was also formed in the state. Read on to find out the answers to these and discover other facts about North Carolina's sports.

This Legendary MLB Player Hit His First Professional Home Run *and* Earned His Famous Nickname in North Carolina

Today, he's a household name and baseball legend. In March of 1914, a legendary MLB player hit his first professional home run in Fayetteville, North Carolina.

That player, George Herman Ruth Jr.—otherwise known as Babe Ruth—hit a long home run during the last inning of the exhibition game. It took place at the Cape Fear Fair Ground.

It was also in Fayetteville that Babe Ruth earned his infamous nickname. Ruth, who was 19 years old at the time, had needed a legal guardian to sign his baseball contract so that he could play at the professional level. The Baltimore Orioles team manager recognized his talent and adopted Ruth so that he could play for the team. It was while the team was in Fayetteville, on their way to spring training in Florida, that they first learned of Ruth's adoption. It was this, along with Ruth's immature behavior of playing on elevators at the Lafayette Hotel, that led them to call him "Dunn's baby." This nickname later got changed to "Babe."

And to think this important part of MLB history started out in Fayetteville, North Carolina!

Only One North Carolinian Sports Team Has Ever Won a Major Title

North Carolina is home to three professional sports teams: the Carolina Panthers (NFL), the Carolina Hurricanes (NHL), and the Charlotte Hornets (NBA). It might surprise you to learn that although there are three major pro sports teams, only *one* of those teams has ever won a major title.

That team would be the Carolina Hurricanes, who won the Stanley Cup back in 2006.

Although the Carolina Panthers have made it to the Super Bowl not just once but *twice*, the team did not win. They have, however, won six division titles, including one in the NFC West and five in the NFC South.

North Carolina's Official State Sport is...

NASCAR! This is because of the sport's history, which is deep rooted in the state. Did you know that, while Daytona may play a key role in the sport's start, NASCAR was *technically* born in North Carolina? The formation of NASCAR all has to do with North Carolina's bootleg moonshine industry!

Former NASCAR driver Robert Glenn Johnson Jr. (who's most often called "Junior Johnson") played a big role in the sport's history. Johnson's ancestors made moonshine since the Whiskey Rebellion. His father was a bootlegger and during the Prohibition era, the family's home was literally stacked with cases of hooch. In 1935, the authorities raided the Johnson's farm and confiscated over 7,000 gallons of whiskey, making the raid the largest seizure of illegal alcohol in the country!

But prior to the raid, Junior Johnson had been a moonshine runner. It was then that he had discovered what a talented driver he was. He had to drive fast to outrun highway patrol or anyone else who would have threatened him from running the moonshine to where it needed to be. Johnson—and other moonshine runners—had to make changes to their vehicles to fly under the radar and drive at high speed on winding backroads.

Johnson himself has said that if it weren't for whiskey, NASCAR never would have been formed.

Moonshining was really common in the rural areas of North Carolina where people did illegal things to pull themselves out of poverty. During the Prohibition era, North Carolina was commonly referred to as the "Moonshine Capital of the World."

With NASCAR's roots seeded deep in North Carolina history, it's no surprise that it was named the official state sport back in 2011.

The NASCAR Hall of Fame is Located in the Tar Heel State

Now that you know that NASCAR was born in North Carolina, it probably won't surprise you to learn that the NASCAR Hall of Fame can also be found in the state.

Located in Charlotte, North Carolina, the NASCAR Hall of Fame honors the history and heritage of the sport. It features a number of artifacts, hands-on exhibits, and a gear shop. At the Glory Road exhibit, you'll find a number of historical race cars and tracks that are significant to the history of the sport. The Hall of Honor is where you'll find the NASCAR Hall of Fame inductees enshrined. There's also a 278-seat High Octane theater where you'll find a film about NASCAR's history. There's also an exhibit called Race Week where you'll get a behind the scenes look at how NASCAR drivers prep for races.

If you're a fan of NASCAR, this is one of North Carolina's sports attractions you won't want to miss out on!

This Major NASCAR Event Takes Place in North Carolina

If you're a NASCAR fan, then you already know the Coca-Cola 600 takes places at the Charlotte Motor Speedway in Concord, North Carolina every Memorial Day Weekend. The race has been happening every year since 1960.

Recognized as one of the most significant races of the sport, the race encompasses 600 miles—making it the longest NASCAR race.

Another one of the unique features about the race is that it changes drastically from beginning to end. When the race begins at 6:30 p.m., there's sunlight for the first third of the race. By the second third, the race takes place at dusk. The final portion is held under lights.

This NASCAR Legend Was From North Carolina

Today, he's widely regarded as one of the greatest NASCAR drivers in history, but his life started out in the Tar Heel State. Did you know that Dale Earnhardt Sr. was born in Kannapolis, North Carolina?

Dale Earnhardt was born into a family of racing. Earnhardt's father, Ralph Earnhardt, was one of the best short-track drivers in North Carolina during his time. During 1956, Ralph Earnhardt won his first (and only) NASCAR Sportsman Championship in Greenville, South Carolina. Dale Earnhardt was five years old at the time.

Despite the fact that Ralph Earnhardt didn't want his son to pursue a career in race car driving, Dale left high school to do so. Ralph taught his son, but he died when of a heart attack when he was just 45 years old. It took a long time for Dale to feel as though he had proven himself to his father, who had been a very hard teacher.

Between his three marriages, Earnhardt had five children, including his son Dale Earnhardt Jr., who also grew up to be a NASCAR sensation.

During the course of his career, Dale Earnhardt Sr. won 76 Winston Cup races (including the Daytona 500 in 1998), and seven NASCAR Winston Cup championship, the most of all-time, which is a record that he ties with Richard Petty and Jimmie Johnson for.

Thanks to his aggressive driving style, Dale Earnhardt Sr. earned several nicknames, the most popular being "The Intimidator." Some of his other nicknames included "The Man in Black" and "The Count of Monte Carlo."

Dale Earnhardt Sr. died in a collision during the final lap of the Daytona 500 in February of 2001. He was inducted into the NASCAR Hall of Fame in 2010.

This NASCAR Champion Also Hails from the State

Did you know that former NASCAR driver and champion Richard Petty is from North Carolina? Petty was born in Level Cross in Randolph County, NC.

Like Dale Earnhardt, Richard Petty was born into a NASCAR family. His father, Lee Petty, was also a driver who won the very first Daytona 500 back in 1959. Lee Petty was a three-time NASCAR champion. Richard Petty's son Kyle was a NASCAR driver, as well as his grandson Adam, who died in a collision at New Hampshire International Speedway in 2000.

Richard Petty, who earned the nickname "The King," won seven NASCAR Championships over the course of his career. Petty also won a record 200 races throughout his career. He won the Daytona 500 seven times and won 27 races, including 10 of which were won consecutively, during the 1967 season alone. He was the first driver to ever win his 500th race, a record that wasn't broken again until Matt Kenseth joined him in 2013. Richard Petty is not only statistically the most accomplished NASCAR driver in history, but he's also one of the most beloved and respected NASCAR drivers of all-time.

Richard Petty was inducted into the NASCAR Hall of Fame back in 2010.

Though Richard Petty retired from NASCAR in 1991, he now operates Richard Petty Motorsports in Level Cross, North Carolina.

The Richard Petty Museum is also located in Level Cross as well. The museum honors the Petty family's NASCAR legacy. The museum has exhibits on Lee Petty and Richard Petty, as well as Richard Petty's NASCAR Hall of Famer cousins, Dale Inman and Maurice Petty.

The Carolina Panthers Weren't the State's First Professional Football Team

You might think the Carolina Panthers were the Tar Heel State's first professional football team, but you'd be wrong. In fact, there were several other professional football teams that played in the state.

There was a team called the Charlotte Bantams who played during the Great Depression. The team played for three seasons before it was discontinued in 1934. Then in 1941, the Dixie League's Charlotte Clippers were established. In the 1970s, the Charlotte Hornets played for World Football League.

We can thank bipartisanship for helping bring the NFL to the Carolinas. Then Republican Senator Jesse Helms of North Carolina and Democratic Senator Ernest Hollings of South Carolina worked together to lobby for an expansion team that would play for their shared region. Thanks to these two politicians' collaborative effort, Charlotte was given a brand-new NFL franchise in October of 1993.

This NBA Legend Grew Up in Wilmington, North Carolina

Today, he's one of the most famous former NBA players of all-time. Did you know that NBA legend Michael Jordan grew up in North Carolina?

Technically, North Carolina isn't his home state. Jordan was born in Brooklyn, New York, but his family moved to Wilmington, North Carolina when he was just a toddler. Michael Jordan went to Emsley A. Laney High School in Wilmington. In addition to high school basketball, Jordan also played baseball and football. Jordan tried out for the school's varsity team when he was a sophomore, but he was turned down because he was too short. (Jordan was 5'11").

Determined to prove that his height wouldn't affect his game, Jordan became the star player of the junior varsity team. Over the course of the following summer, he also grew four inches.

When Michael Jordan was a senior, he was chosen to play for the McDonald's All-American Team.

He was recruited by a number of college basketball programs, some of which included Duke, Syracuse, North Carolina, South Carolina, and Virginia. Michael Jordan chose to attend the University of North Carolina at Chapel Hill, which he attended on a basketball scholarship.

While he was attending UNC at Chapel Hill, Jordan was named the ACC Freshman of the Year. He made the winning shot in the NCAA Championship game against Georgetown in 1982. Jordan later went on to describe the winning shot at the turning point of his basketball career. He was also chosen for the NCAA All-American First Team during his sophomore and junior years. Jordan was also won the awards for both the Naismith and the Wooden College Player of the Year in 1984.

A year before Michael Jordan was supposed to graduate from UNC, he left the university to enter the NBA draft in 1984. The Chicago Bulls selected him as their 3rd overall pick. Michael Jordan played the next 15 seasons the Chicago Bulls and Washington Wizards.

And to think that Michael Jordan's basketball career started out in Wilmington, North Carolina!

The Charlotte Hornets Weren't the State's First Professional Basketball Team

It might surprise you to learn that the Charlotte Hornets were *not* North Carolina's first professional basketball team. The first pro basket team in the state was actually the Carolina Cougars, who were a part of the American Basketball Association league. The Cougars played between the years of 1969 and 1974.

Today's Charlotte Hornets Aren't the Original Team

It might also surprise you to learn that the Charlotte Hornets that play today aren't the original Charlotte Hornets. The team wasn't always called the Hornets. In fact, the team lost its name for 10 years!

The original Charlotte Hornets team was established by the NFL back in 1988 as an expansion team. In 2002, however, the team moved to New Orleans and changed its name to the New Orleans Hornets.

In 2004, Charlotte got a new franchise, which it called the Bobcats. It was recognized as a new expansion team at the time. Then in 2013, the New Orleans

Hornets decided to rebrand themselves and the team was renamed the New Orleans Pelicans instead. They returned the original Hornets name to Charlotte. During the 2014/2015 season, the Bobcats changed their name back to the Charlotte Hornets.

The Charlotte Hornets Are Owned by…

Michael Jordan! Although Jordan never played for the Charlotte Hornets himself, he does own the team today. Jordan acquired the controlling majority of the team back in 2010. At the time of the acquisition, the team was still known as the Charlotte Bobcats.

Fun fact: The Hornets are the only team in all of the NBA that doesn't have the Nike logo as their jersey logo. Have you ever wondered why that is? It all has to do with Michael Jordan's ownership of the team. The Hornets have the "Jumpman" logo, instead of the Nike logo. The Jumpman logo is owned by Nike and is used to promote the Air Jordan brand.

This Former Boxer is From the Tar Heel State

Did you know that former professional boxer "Sugar" Ray Leonard is from North Carolina? The former professional boxer was born in Wilmington, NC.

Born Ray Charles Leonard, he was named after his mother's favorite singer, Ray Charles. The family moved to Washington, D.C. when Leonard was just three years old and then later to Maryland when he was 10 years old.

Leonard was a part of "The Fabulous Four," which was a group of boxers who fought each other during the 1980s. The others were Roberto Durán, Thomas Hearns and Marvin Hagler. The Fabulous Four helped popularize the lower weight classes, which helped spark a newfound interest in boxing during the post-Muhammed Ali era.

Sugar Ray Leonard's nickname came about when Sarge Johnson, the U.S. Olympic Boxing Team assistant coach, said he was "sweet as sugar." The nickname caught on but soon evolved into "Sugar Ray" after Sugar Ray Robinson, who is considered to be the best boxer in history.

Over the course of his career, which spanned from 1977 to 1997, Leonard won numerous titles. These included world titles in five weight divisions, the undisputed welterweight title, and the lineal championship in three weight divisions.

Leonard became the first boxer to earn over $100 million in purses. In the 1980s, he was named the "Boxer of the Decade" and was later inducted into the International Boxing Hall of Fame.

Today, Sugar Ray Leonard is often considered one of the greatest boxers in history. In 2002, *The Ring* named Leonard the No. 9 greatest fighter of the last 80 years.

Michael Jordan Isn't the Only Tar Heels Alumni Who Went on to Achieve Athletic Success

While Michael Jordan may be the most famous athlete to have ever attended the University of North Carolina, he's not the only Tar Heels alumni who went on to achieve athletic success. A number of other athletes also started their athletic careers out at the college. Some of these include:

- **Mia Hamm** – Former professional soccer player Mia Hamm attended the University of North Carolina at Chapel Hill from 1989 to 1993. During that time, she helped the Tar Heels win four NCAA Division I Women's Soccer Championships. Hamm went on to win two Olympic gold medals and two FIFA Women's World Cup championships. Hamm played as forward for the U.S. women's national soccer team and later played for the Washington Freedom of the Women's United Soccer Association (WUSA). Hamm was recognized as a women's soccer icon and was the face of WUSA.

- **Davis Milton Love III** – Professional golfer Davis Milton Love III played golf at the University of North Carolina at Chapel Hill. Over the course of his college golf career, Love won six titles, including the ACC tournament championship. Love has gone on to win 21 events on the PGA Tour, including the PGA Championship in 1997. He also won the 1992 and 2003 Players Championship. In 2017, Love was inducted into the World Golf Hall of Fame.

- **B.J. Surhoff** – Former MLB player B.J. Surhoff is a University of North Carolina at Chapel Hill alumni. During his time there, he played on the first U.S. Olympic baseball team. He later went on to play the Milwaukee Brewers, Baltimore Orioles, and Atlanta Braves.

- **Marion Jones** – Former track and field athlete and basketball player Marion Jones attended UNC. She went on to win three gold medals and two bronze medals during the 2000 Summer Olympics, but they were later revoked after Jones admitted to steroid use. Jones also played for the Tulsa Shock in the Women's National Basketball Association.

North Carolina is a Golfing Hotspot

North Carolina might not be the first name that comes to mind when you think of golf, but the state is actually a golfing hotspot!

Pinehurst Resort is a famous golf resort located in the Sandhills. The resort has hosted several major golf championships. Some of these golf championships include the United States Open Championship, the PGA Championship, and the Ryder Cup Matches. In 2014, the resort gained recognition when its most famous course, No. 2, hosted the U.S. Opens for both men *and* women in the same year.

There are also several professional golf tours that make stops in the state each year. These include the EGolf Professional Tour, the Annual PGA Tour, the Quail Hollow Championship, and the Greater Greensboro Open. The Carolina Classic also takes place in Raleigh each year.

The North Carolina Sports Hall of Fame Honors Athletes from the Tar Heel State

The North Carolina Sports Hall of Fame was established in 1963. Located in Charlotte, the Hall of Fame honors athletes from the state, as well as those who have brought recognition to the state of North Carolina.

Some of the artifacts you can find at the North Carolina Sports Hall of Fame include the following:

- Richard Petty's race car
- Dale Earnhardt's fire suit
- Arnold Palmer's Ryder Cup golf bag
- Meadowlark Lemon's Harlem Globetrotter's basketball uniform
- Charlie "Choo Choo" Justice's college football jersey

- Kay Yow's Olympic team basketball

RANDOM FACTS

1. Legendary golf player Arnold Palmer went to Wake Forest University in Winston-Salem, North Carolina where he played golf.

2. North Carolina isn't home to a Major League Baseball Team. It is, however, home to several minor league and summer collegiate summer league teams, including the Charlotte Knights, the Durham Bulls, and the Carolina Mudcats.

3. The Carolina Panthers could have been named the "Cobras," "Rhinos," or "Cougars." These names were all considered. The team's franchise owner Jerry Richardson chose "Panthers" because his son Mark had always liked the wild black cats.

4. The Carolina Hurricanes were once known as the Hartford Whalers. The team moved from Hartford, Connecticut to North Carolina in 1997, which is when they changed their name to the Hurricanes.

5. Panthers player Cam Newton was the first NFL quarterback to ever have a minimum of 3,000 passing yards and 500 rushing yards in five consecutive seasons.

6. The Carolina Panthers logo represents the outline of North and South Carolina. If you tilt your head, you might be able to see it.

7. Championship golfer Charles Sifford, who is a Charlotte native, helped desegregate the PGA.

8. The late MLB player James "Catfish" Hunter was born and raised in Hertford, North Carolina. Hunter pitched for the Kansas City Athletics, the Oakland Athletics, and the New York Yankees. He was one of the first pitchers to win 200 games before he was 31. Hunter was inducted into the National Baseball Hall of Fame. Bob Dylan wrote a song about him called "Catfish."

9. The late baseball player Walter "Buck" Leonard, who is known as the "Black Lou Gehrig," played as a first baseman for the Homestead Grays in the negro leagues. Buck Leonard grew up in Rocky Mount, North Carolina. Buck Leonard never played for the MLB. He did, however, turn down an MLB contract because he believed he was too old. Buck Leonard was inducted into the National Baseball Hall of Fame.

10. Former NASCAR driver and commentator Dale Jarrett was born and raised in Conover, North Carolina. In 1996, Jarrett became the first driver to ever win the Daytona 500 and Brickyard 400 during the same season. He was inducted into the NASCAR Hall of Fame.

11. Former NBA player Walter Davis is from Pineville, North Carolina. He played for the Phoenix Suns during the majority of his NBA career. He also played for the U.S. Olympic basketball team in 1976, which won a gold medal.

12. Snowboarder Seth Wescott is a two-time Olympic gold medalist. Wescott is from Durham, North Carolina.

13. Competitive swimmer Ricky Berens was born and raised in Charlotte, North Carolina. Berens is a two-time Olympic gold medalist and holds the record for the 4 x 200-meter freestyle relay.

14. Lowell Bailey, who is from Siler City, North Carolina, holds several athletic records. He was the first U.S. biathlete champion. He was also the oldest individual gold medalist in biathlon history when he won at 35 years old.

15. Speed skater and U.S. Olympic competitor Heather Bergsma is from High Point, North Carolina.

16. Michael Jordan may be one of the most famous athletes to grow up in North Carolina, but he wasn't included in the North Carolina Sports Hall of Fame for many years. Even though he selected for induction, Jordan hadn't been able to attend the required banquet for induction. Jordan was inducted in 2010. His ceremony was held

during halftime at a Charlotte Bobcats game, which he already owned at the time.

17. Former NFL player Sonny Jurgensen was born and raised in Wilmington, North Carolina. Jurgensen was the quarterback for the Philadelphia Eagles and the Washington Redskins. He was inducted into the Pro Football Hall of Fame.

18. Former NBA star James Worthy is from Gastonia, North Carolina. Worthy is considered one of the best NBA players in history. Today, he's a commentator, host, and analyst.

19. Late MLB player Enos Slaughter played for the St. Louis Cardinals. Slaughter was from Roxboro, North Carolina.

20. Pro golfer Ray Floyd is from Fort Bragg, North Carolina. Floyd has won many tournaments on the PGA Tour and Senior PGA Tour. He's a World Golf Hall of Famer.

Test Yourself – Questions

1. The only North Carolina professional sports team to win a major title is:

   a. The Carolina Panthers
   b. The Carolina Hornets
   c. The Carolina Hurricanes

2. Michael Jordan owns which of North Carolina's sports teams?

   a. The Carolina Panthers
   b. The Charlotte Hornets
   c. The Carolina Hurricanes

3. Which NASCAR legend was _not_ born in North Carolina?

   a. Richard Petty
   b. Dale Earnhardt Sr.
   c. Dale Earnhardt Jr.

4. The state sport of North Carolina is:

   a. NASCAR
   b. Basketball
   c. Football

5. Babe Ruth hit his first home run and gained his famous nickname in which North Carolina town?

   a. Fayetteville
   b. Fort Bragg
   c. Charlotte

Answers

1. c.
2. b.
3. c.
4. a.
5. a.

CHAPTER SIX

NORTH CAROLINA'S URBAN LEGENDS, UNSOLVED MYSTERIES, AND OTHER WEIRD FACTS!

Every state has its fair share of strange occurrences, unsolved mysteries, and creepy places. Do you know about the urban legends that haunt the state of North Carolina? With its Cherokee population, there's plenty of folklore surrounding the state. Do you know about the Cherokee fairies that are believed to live in the southern Appalachian Mountains? Have you heard about some of the state's greatest unsolved mysteries? Did you know that there's a place in North Carolina that's believed to be a favorite spot of the Devil? Warning: This chapter may give you goosebumps. To learn about these and other weird facts of North Carolina, read on!

The Mystery Beast of Bladenboro

The Beast of Bladenboro is one of the most popular urban legends that haunt the state of North Carolina. Also sometimes referred to the Legend of the Vampiric, the urban legend is also considered by many to be one of the state's biggest mysteries.

The earliest report of the beast dates back to 1953. A woman living in the town of Bladenboro allegedly heard her neighbors' dogs barking and making pained sounds. When she went to make sure the dogs were okay, she saw a large creature that looked like a cat sauntering away into the darkness of the night.

During the following days, six more dogs were reportedly killed. Most of the dogs had broken jaws and all of them had been drained of their blood. One of the dogs had even been decapitated.

People thought the dogs were killed by a vampiric beast that lived in the woods. They attempted to hunt the creature. The legendary creature thus became known as "Vampiric."

As panic ensued, more and more people began to report seeing the Beast of Bladenboro.

Then in 1954, a human was attacked by what had resembled a large feline-like creature, which eventually fled into the woods.

People in the town had grown hysterical. They wanted to hunt the creature. The Mayor of Bladenboro and the chief of police wanted to put an end to the panic, so they allegedly killed a bobcat and hung its body in the town square, claiming that they had caught the beast. Interestingly, the Beast of Bladenboro stopped attacks after this.

So, what exactly was the Beast of Bladenboro? The TV series *MonsterQuest* on *The History Channel* investigated the state's most famous beast. They believed that the attack may have been a cougar. Some people believe that the Vampiric may have been a black panther or even a Chupacabra. However, it's unlikely that the world will ever really know what creature was responsible for all of those attacks.

Some who have claimed to see the beast say that there's no way it was just an animal. One man who called the *Observer* said he saw the beast's corpse when he was just seven years old and that he will never forget the impact it had on him.

Today, the town of Bladenboro holds a Beast Fest every year in honor of this eerie piece of the town's history.

The Legend of the Devil's Tramping Ground

Have you ever heard the legend of the Devil's Tramping Ground? It's one of North Carolina's most famous—and most creepy—legends.

Legends of the Devil's Tramping Ground have been passed down for at least 200 years. Located in a forest near the town of Bennett, North Carolina, there's a 40-foot circle of ground where nothing grows. There are no trees, no bushes—not even a single blade of grass. The ground is said to be burnt and lifeless and rumor has it that nothing has grown in that circle for hundreds of years, even though plenty of vegetation surrounds the circle.

So, what's so eerie about this circle of bare ground? Well, local lore says that the reason it doesn't grow is because the Devil "tramps" around the circle as he makes evil plots and plans. Some even believe this spot is where the Devil manifests to wreak havoc on Earth. It's thought to be somewhat of a gateway from Hell to North Carolina.

It has been said that anything that's left in the circle overnight mysteriously moves outside of the circle by the time morning comes. Dogs refuse to even enter these alleged unholy grounds. Perhaps the eeriest part of the legends is the alleged animal sacrifices. It has been said that carcasses of dead animals have been found scattered in the woods near the circle.

And if you're thinking about staying there overnight, you should probably think twice about that. According to the legend, trespassers are said to witness events that will drive them insane. The campers who have dared spend the night near the

Devil's Tramping Ground have claimed to see the Devil walk the Earth. It has been said that many of those campers have never fully recovered from their experience, with many of them spending the rest of their lives in mental institutions.

The Unsolved Be-Lo Murders

The Be-Lo Murders is one of the most chilling cold cases in North Carolina. To date, it remains one of North Carolina's biggest unsolved mysteries.

It all started out on a warm summer night in June of 1993 in the small town of Windsor. At 6 p.m., the Be-Lo Supermarket, which was located on South Granville Street, closed. Not long after, 9-1-1 was called due to the horrendous crime that took place inside the store. When Windsor Police arrived on the scene, they found blood everywhere.

So, what happened that tragic day?

A man had been hiding in the store at closing time. Once all of the customers were gone, he approached the manager of the store, Grover "Bud" Cecil, and stole more than $3,000 from him. The robber proceeded to escort Cecil and Joyce Reason, the store cashier, to the back of the store. The robber forced Cecil to summon a four-person cleaning crew, which had arrived when the store closed, to join him at the back of the store.

Once all of the people in the store had been gathered in the same area, the robber forced Cecil to use duct tape to bound the other victim's hands. The robber then duct-taped Cecil's hands.

This is where the tragedy began. The robber stacked the victims on the floor in three two-person piles. He proceeded to shoot the person on top of each pile (Cecil, Reason, and Johnnie Rankins of the cleaning crew). He also injured another person, Sylvester "Tony" Welch, who survived.

When the killer's handgun jammed on the fourth shot, he rolled each victim onto their stomachs. He went to a back room of the store, returning with a knife that he used to stab a fifth victim (cleaning crew worker Jasper Hardy) in the throat and back. He stabbed him so hard in the back that the knife broke. The killer didn't harm the sixth victim—Thomas Hardy of the cleaning crew.

After the attacks were over, the killer grabbed the stolen money, the knife, and the keys and left the store.

Once the killer was gone, Welch crawled to the front of the store to call for help, dragging blood across the store from the gunshot wound he had endured.

The killer was described as being a black male with a medium complexion. He was said to have a slender build and stood 6' to 6'2" tall. He had a military-style haircut.

The Be-Lo shut down shortly after the tragedy took place.

To this day, the Be-Lo Murders Killer was never found. No one knows the motive. The case remains open to this day, with a $30,000 reward still being offered for information that may lead to the killer's arrest and conviction.

The Legend of the Lake Norman Monster

North Carolina might not be the first place that comes to mind when you think of lake monsters. However, North Carolina is said to have its own version of the Lochness Monster.

Normie is said to haunt Lake Norman. There have been frequent alleged sightings of the Lake Norman Monster, which is often described as a 20-foot long, serpent-like creature. Some claim it has scaly fins or flippers. Descriptions and size of the reported monster sometimes vary.

The lake monster has been said to chase boats and comes close to swimmers and water skiers. Although in some reports Normie is said to be friendly, there have also allegedly been attacks. One scuba driver reported an attack from a creature with a doglike head and red eyes that chomped one of his flippers. While the diver survived the attack, the flipper was never recovered.

Another report of the monster came from a jet skier, who claimed that the monster brushed against his leg, leaving behind a slimy residue. The jet skier claimed the slime left him with an itchy rash.

There's something that sets Normie apart from many other lake monsters. Many lake monsters are believed to be prehistoric creatures that have somehow managed to survive. But Lake Norman is a manmade lake that was built in 1963, which makes it unlikely that Normie could be a prehistoric creature. Some believe that Normie may be an overgrown garfish, freshwater eel, catfish, or bowfin. Others think the monster could be either an alligator or a type of salamander known as a "hellbender," which can be two feet in length. Then there are some who think Normie might also be a mutant fish created by pollution from the local nuclear plant.

No matter what Normie is, the creature has drawn interest from cryptozoologists and underwater investigators throughout the world. The lake monster has been featured on *America's Monsters and Boogeymen*, *River Monsters*, and *Deadliest Catch*.

The Mystery of the Brown Mountain Lights

The Brown Mountain Lights are one of North Carolina's most famous unexplained phenomena. In fact, they're one of the most famous and mysterious natural phenomena in all of America.

The lights, which often appear red, blue or yellow in color and tend to be formed in a spherical shape, tend to move across the sky and then disappear or explode without making any sounds Some people have reported an electric-like surge from this alleged explosion. The lights appear at random intervals over the top of Brown Mountain. They're generally visible at a distance but tend to vanish when you climb the mountain. They're said to be twice the size of a star and sometimes form in swarms.

The lights have become a tourist attraction, with people coming from all over the country to see the mysterious lights. The lights are most often seen between September and early November.

The lights have been seen for at least 100 years, with one of the earliest accounts dating back to September of 1913 when a fisherman reported seeing red, circular lights. After the report was made, a Geological Survey employee investigated the area and concluded that the witness had actually seen train lights.

This theory doesn't hold up, however. Soon after the investigation, a massive flood hit the area, causing power outages and trains to stop running for a while after. Several bridges were even washed out from the flood. During this time, the Brown Mountain Lights continued to be seen.

So, if train lights aren't the cause of the Brown Mountain Lights, what is? No one knows, but plenty of theories abound. Some people, including scientists, think the lights may be caused by swamp gas (even though there are no nearby swamps or marshes). Others attribute them to the spirits of the Native American warriors killed in battle and the lost souls of their maidens, which stems from Indian folklore that dates back to 1200 A.D. According to one local legend, the lights are the result of a woman who was murdered by her adulterous husband in the mountains.

In 1967, a scientist suggested that the lights were caused by nitrous-based vapors that were being emitted from the mountain. No one has ever proved or disproved this theory to be accurate.

Still, it's a mystery that plagues scientists to this day. No one knows the cause of Brown Mountain Lights, but the mystery phenomena have been featured in episodes of *Mystery Hunters*, *Weird or What?*, and *Ancient Aliens*. It was also the basis of the 2014 movie *Alien Abduction*. Even author Nicholas Sparks drew inspiration from the lights in his only paranormal novel *True Believer*.

The Cryptozoology & Paranormal Museum is Located in North Carolina

Did you know the Cryptozoology & Paranormal Museum is located in Littleton, North Carolina?

According to the museum's website, it's dedicated to:

- Artifacts and information about Bigfoot.
- Evidence of ghosts, and paranormal investigation.
- Local stories and evidence about ghosts and cryptids.
- Lake and river monsters.
- Evidence and stories about UFOs.
- Famous Fakes (e.g. the Fiji Mermaid).

The museum hosts "Bigfoot in the Park." You can visit Medoc Mountain State Park in Hollister, North Carolina, which is where many alleged Bigfoot sightings have taken place and tracks have been found.

The museum also hosts walking tours and ghost hunts through the Historic District of Littleton.

The Ghost of Blackbeard May Haunt Teach's Hole

Teach's Hole on Ocracoke Island is one of the most popular tourist destinations for anyone wanting to learn more about the Outer Banks' most famous pirate, Blackbeard. But did you know that Teach's Hole is believed to be haunted by Blackbeard himself?

Teach's Hole is the spot where Blackbeard was captured for the crimes he had committed. It was where he was beheaded. His head was allegedly hung from the ship's bowsprit as proof that he had been conquered.

According to legend, Blackbeard screamed *after* his decapitated head had been hung from the ship. His body, which had been thrown overboard, allegedly "swam" (or circled) around Maynard's ship three times before it eventually sunk.

Today, some say that at night, you may see his decapitated body swimming in the cove or walking the beaches in a continuous search of his head.

Some people claim that you can hear Blackbeard's voice calling out from the hidden cove on stormy nights. People have reportedly heard a noise that sounds a lot like a pained person screaming out, "Where's my head?"

Others claim that Blackbeard's ghost appears in the form of a strange light beneath the water in the cove. People think that light is thought to be Blackbeard's spirit, swimming through the waters as he looks for his head.

The Odd Disappearance of Nell Cropsey

The disappearance of Nell Cropsey remains one of North Carolina's biggest unsolved mysteries. The disappearance drew nationwide attention. Although one man was even convicted of her murder, there are plenty of question's surrounding Cropsey's mysterious death.

In November of 1901, a 19-year-old woman named Ella "Nell" Cropsey went missing from her home in Elizabeth City, North Carolina.

Nell Cropsey was not only a very attractive young woman, but she was also from a very wealthy family. Shortly after moving to Elizabeth City from Brooklyn with her family 1898, Nell had drawn the attention of many potential suitors.

At the time of her disappearance, Nell Cropsey had been courting a man named Jim Wilcox for nearly three years. However, Nell was allegedly growing frustrated with Wilcox because he hadn't yet proposed to her. As a result of her frustrations, she had begun to flirt with other men to try to encourage Wilcox to propose.

Nell's plan seemed to have backfired, however. In November of 1901, she and Wilcox ended up getting into an argument at the Cropsey family's home. Nell's family had overheard them yelling at one another, but they couldn't make out what the argument was over. Her family said that Nell and Jim had seemed to make up, but no one knew for sure if they had fully resolved their argument.

Around 11 p.m. that night, Nell and Wilcox stepped outside. It was the last time Nell Cropsey had ever been seen alive.

After Wilcox left, Nell's sister, Ollie Cropsey, had heard a banging sound at the back of the house. Ollie went outside and discovered that the screen door was broken. There was no sign of who or what may have broken the door. Ollie then went upstairs to find out if Nell was in her room, but she wasn't. While this made Ollie uneasy, she went to sleep anyway.

Not long after Ollie had gone to sleep, a neighbor started yelling that someone was trying to steal the Cropsey's family pig. This woke up the entire family. When they got downstairs, they realized three things: 1). Nell still hadn't come home yet, 2). The front door had been left wide open, and 3). The umbrella that Nell had given to Jim Wilcox was next to the front door, and none of the family members remembered seeing it there earlier in the night.

The following morning, Nell still hadn't returned home. The police were called and a search began. The entire town was searched, but there were no signs of Nell anywhere.

The initial suspect was Jim Wilcox, of course. Wilcox claimed that he didn't know what had happened to Nell. The police didn't believe him, however. Wilcox was arrested as a suspect.

At the end of December, more than a month after she had gone missing, Nell's body was found floating in the Pasquotank River. Mrs. Cropsey was the one who spotted something floating in the river. She sent some boatmen out, who confirmed her fears. At the time, Jim Wilcox was still being held at the local jail.

It wasn't just mere intuition that had led Mrs. Cropsey to the river, however. A few days before her daughter's body was discovered, the Cropsey family had received a letter with a New York postmark that listed a detailed account of the events that had taken place the night Nell had gone missing. According to the letter writer, Nell had stopped a "vagrant" from stealing the family pig. The writer claimed that the man had grabbed a stick, which he'd used to knock Nell unconscious and then carried her to the Pasquotank River where he stole a boat. The writer claimed the man had rowed out into the river to dump Nell's body and provided a map of where her body could be found. Nell's body was, indeed, found near the spot on the map. To this day, it's unknown who sent the letter and if the events contained in the letter were true.

When Nell Cropsey's body was discovered, the town of Elizabeth City was infuriated. A lynch mob went to the jail and demanded that Jim Wilcox be released to them. The Cropsey family tried to convince the crowd to let justice be determined in the courtroom. Governor Aycock eventually had to send in a small naval reserve group to break up the crowd.

Jim Wilcox went on trial and was convicted of murder. He was sentence to 30 years in prison. The courtroom cheered for the prosecution.

Then in 1918, the governor at the time pardoned Wilcox.

Later in life, Wilcox claimed that he knew how Nell Cropsey died, but he carried his secret to the grave.

So, who *did* kill Nell? While Wilcox may have done it, a lot of people didn't think he could have had time to dump her body in the river when he was arrested so soon after she went missing. Some thought Nell may have killed herself, but she didn't leave a note.

Two major factors compounding the case were poor detective work and an unprofessional autopsy, which was performed in the Cropsey's barn in front of curious people watching.

Unfortunately, the world will probably never know who killed Nell Cropsey.

People who have lived in the former Cropsey home have reported paranormal activity. Some have claimed to see the apparition of a pale young woman.

It's believed that Nell's spirit lingers in the home, unable to rest due to her tragic past and lack of justice being served.

The Strange Blood Showers of North Carolina

The blood showers of Sampson County and Chatham County may be the most bizarre thing that has ever happened in North Carolina. Warning: This is a little gory.

The first documented case of blood and flesh falling from the sky took place in February of 1850 on a farm owned by Thomas Clarkson in Sampson County. Clarkson's account of the flesh fall and a sample were taken to Fayetteville by a man named Mr. Holland.

Clarkson reported flesh and blood, 250 or 300 yards in length. He believed the contents contained flesh, liver, brains, and blood. Three of Clarkson's children were there to witness it, as well as a neighbor. Clarkson reported a red cloud overhead just prior to the blood shower.

The sample provided by Mr. Holland confirmed that it was, indeed, flesh and blood. It wasn't known what type of animal the sample had come from, however.

Then in February of 1884, a woman named Kit Lasater reported a second blood shower in Chatham County. Lasater was the wife of a black tenant farmer who lived on a farm belonging to Silas Beckworth.

Kit Lasater had been standing in a field that had just been plowed when blood fell from the sky.

After word of the incident spread, people came to the field to check out the ground. A rectangular area spanning about 60 feet in circumference, as well as some tree branches, had been covered in splotches that resembled blood. A reputable physician in the area confirmed that it was blood.

Dr. Sidney Atwater took a sample of the material, which he took to a chemistry professor named Dr. Francis Preston Venable at the University of North Carolina for examination. While Venable and his colleagues were amused by the sample at first, Venable came up with a theory. He first attributed the material to the wind and plowed land.

However, after he performed chemical, spectrographic, and microscopic tests, Dr. Venable concluded that the sample *did* contain blood. He was unsure what type of blood it was, though.

He suggested that a bird may have flown over the area and dropped its bleeding prey, though he noted that a lot of blood must have fallen for it to cover such a large area of land. Venable questioned if it could have been a prank or hoax.

One of the most peculiar parts about this whole incident is that these blood showers happened *before* Wilbur and Orville Wright made their first successful flight.

The Unsolved Murder of Debbie Wolfe

Back in December of 1985, one of the most mysterious deaths took place in North Carolina.

A young nurse named Debbie Wolfe disappeared after she left work. The day before, Wolfe had celebrated Christmas with her family.

When Debbie didn't show up to work on the 27th, her family became worried. Her mom Jenny, her stepdad John, and a family friend named Kevin Gorton went to the cabin where Debbie lived near Fayetteville, North Carolina.

Debbie wasn't anywhere to be found, but something was off.

Debbie was known for being extremely neat and organized. When her family entered the cabin, they were shocked to find that her car was in a different parking spot than it usually was. There were beer cans strewn across her yard, her two dogs hadn't been fed, her uniform had been left on the kitchen floor, and her purse had been shoved behind her bed.

An odd message had also been left on Debbie's answering machine. The caller had said that Debbie had been gone from work for several days. This was false, however, as Debbie had been working at the hospital the previous day.

Her family searched near the pond in her backyard, but there was no sign of Debbie.

Jenny tried to report her daughter as a missing person, but the sheriff's office wouldn't begin an investigation until after 72 hours had passed. They didn't end up beginning an investigation until five days after Debbie had gone missing.

On New Year's Day, Jenny took matters into her own hands. She had Kevin Gorton and another man named Gordon Childress dive into the pond in search of Jenny.

Childress located footprints and drag marks at the bottom of the pond within minutes. He followed the tracks until they led him to Debbie's body. Her body had been placed in a burn barrel. At that point, police were called to the scene to remove her body from the water.

An autopsy was performed, which found that there had been no drugs or alcohol in her system. The cause of death was ruled to be drowning. However, Kevin Gorton didn't believe that Debbie had drowned. Gorton said that drowning victims typically have their eyes and mouth open, as well as outstretched arms and hands. Debbie's body wasn't found in this condition. Wolfe's body was also clean, even though the pond was dirty, leading him to believe she hadn't been swimming in it.

Police investigators felt that her death had been an accident. They believed that she had fallen into the pond while she was playing with her dogs.

Wolfe's family and friends felt that her death hadn't been an accident. They felt that her body being found in a barrel was proof of this. The police investigators claimed that there had never been a barrel and suggested that the divers had actually seen her jacket ballooned out from being submerged in water. The divers were certain of what they had seen. Additionally, a barrel had been missing from Debbie's property.

A few months later, Jenny also noticed that the clothes Debbie hadn't been wearing probably weren't hers. They were too large, with both the bra cup and shoe size being *three times* too large. The police, however, claimed that the clothes belonged to Debbie.

Two potential suspects had been investigated. Debbie had been in charge of the volunteers at the hospital. Two of them had tried to become romantically involved with her. One of the volunteers, who had a history of psychiatric illness, had often asked Debbie out. He had called her and, allegedly claiming to know where she lived, threatened to visit her. The police investigated this volunteer, but he had an alibi and had refused to take a polygraph. Suspiciously, the man left the state a few days later.

A second volunteer, who had also tried to initiate a relationship with Debbie during the weeks leading up to her death, was also questioned by the police.

Jenny believed that this man had left the message on Debbie's answering machine. Though this volunteer was also questioned by the police, they didn't find any evidence linking him to the crime.

To this day, Debbie Wolfe's death remains a mystery. Jenny has since died, so she'll never know who killed her daughter.

The Ghost Ship Found Off the Coast of North Carolina

One of the most mysterious ship incidents in America took place off the coast of North Carolina in 1921.

The *Carroll A. Deering* was a commercial schooner that was found off the coast of Cape Hatteras. The Coast Guard discovered the ship, but they weren't able to reach it for four days. Once they finally arrived, they found almost everything missing. Though dinner had been cooking on the stove, the ship's crew had disappeared completely.

While the U.S. Government investigated what may have happened to the ship, it turned out not to find any definitive answers. The investigation ended in 1922.

There have been a number of theories of what happened to the ship and everyone on it, however.

Some believe that the *Carroll A. Deering* was a victim

of the supernatural Bermuda Triangle. The first time this was ever mentioned as a theory was in Charles Fort's 1931 book *Lo!* However, there are a number of arguments in regards to why this couldn't be true. Although the vessel sailed in the area that's believed to be a part of the Bermuda Triangle, the ship was found several hundred miles away from it. And *if* the Bermuda Triangle were to blame, then why didn't the entire ship go missing?

Hurricanes were considered as a possible theory that the U.S. Government, including the Weather Bureau, believed may have been the cause of the disappearances. However, this theory falls short because the *Deering* had been traveling *away* from the hurricanes' paths. The ship had also been left in an orderly state, which you wouldn't have expected if it had been an emergency evacuation.

Piracy is often thought to be the most likely cause of the *Deering*'s disappearance. This theory was supported by the Captain of the Marine Shipping Board at the time. It was theorized that a group of pirates were responsible for the crew's disappearance. That being said, no pirate suspects were ever named and this was theory was never proven or disproven.

Whatever happened to the *Carroll A. Deering*, it's one of the biggest mysteries to haunt the United States.

The Legend of Peter Dromgoogle is UNC at Chapel Hill's Most Famous Campus Urban Legend

The legend of Peter Dromgoogle is a popular campus tale at the University of North Carolina at Chapel Hill. Peter Dromgoogle was a student at the university back in 1832 before he was killed as the result of an alleged duel.

The story goes like this: Dromgoogle was allegedly in love with a girl named Fannie. However, he wasn't the only one. There was another student, who remains unnamed, who was attending to the university who also had his heart set on Fannie. The other student told Peter he wanted to duel him for Fannie's love. The two agreed to meet at Piney Point, where this battle would take place. Word of the fight began to travel on campus, leading a crowd of people to gather as spectators.

Fannie didn't hear about the duel until it was about to begin. By the time she arrived at Piney Point, Peter had allegedly been shot in the heart. He had fallen onto a large boulder, which just so happened to be the same boulder where he and Fannie had first met and had continued to secretly see one another.

The people who watched the duel take place allegedly buried Peter's body and covered it with the boulder. It's been said that this is where Peter's body remains to this day. That boulder is known as "Dromgoogle Rock" today. It's been said that if you look close enough, you'll still see Peter's blood on the rock.

According to legend, Fannie died the following summer because she was so heartbroken over her true love's death. It's often said that both Fannie and Peter haunt the Dromgoogle Rock and Gimgoul Castle today.

So, how much of this story is true? It's hard to say. It's worth noting that Dromgoogle Rock *does* exist. It can be found at Piney Point, which is located on the property of Gimgoul Castle. However, the boulder cannot be accessed by the general public.

The Biltmore Estate May Be One of the Most Haunted Spots in North Carolina

Few places in North Carolina are believed to be more haunted than the Biltmore Estate. Although the largest home in America is one of Asheville's biggest attractions, it's also believed to be booming with paranormal activity. Some even consider it to be one of the most haunted locations in not only North Carolina but all of America.

The most obvious ghosts that haunt the estate are its previous owners. George Vanderbilt, the former owner of the Biltmore Estate, died on the estate during the 1900s. After his death, his wife Edith allegedly spent a lot of time in the library of the estate (which had been George's favorite place in the house), where she talked to her husband. People have reported hearing the husband and wife whispering to one another in the library.

Some people have also claimed to hear Edith calling out George's name throughout the rest of the estate.

One of the spirits is also said to be that of a headless orange cat that wanders the property of the estate. There have been numerous reports of the feline, who's frequently seen roaming the gardens.

There have also been claims of voices in the swimming pool room. People have also heard unexplained splashes and laughing coming from the pool. Interestingly enough, Edith Vanderbilt was known for throwing pool parties.

The Shadow of the Bear on Whiteside Mountain

Whiteside Mountain is one of the oldest mountains in the world, but what draws many tourists to it is a strange, unexplained natural phenomenon that happens at the mountain each year.

Every fall, the Shadow of the Bear appears on the Whiteside Mountain appears as the sun sets. The bear's shadow looks as though it's rising from the valley below the mountain.

What's interesting about the shadow is that it's said to take the form of several different animals before morphing into the Shadow of the Bear. As the sun descends into the sky, the shadow is said to appear as a tadpole, turtle, cat, dog, mouse, weasel or groundhog, depending on who's interpreting the shadow. Most can agree, however, that in its final form, it looks like a bear.

No one knows for sure what causes this bizarre natural phenomenon to occur. Some consider it one of North Carolina's greatest mysteries. According to old Cherokee legend, the shadow is actually the spirit of a black bear.

The Shadow of the Bear is visible between 5:30 and 6 p.m. from the middle of October until early November near the town of Cashiers, North Carolina. The shadow also appears for a short time in mid-February.

There Are Lots of Legends About North Carolina's Most Haunted Road

Payne Road in Rural Hall, North Carolina is said to be extremely haunted. In fact, it's considered to be the most haunted road in the state. While it's unsure what exactly happened on the road, most believe that something terrifying did happen there. There are a few different stories that explain why the road may be haunted.

The first, most common story is that Edward Payne owned a large slave plantation on the road. His daughter fell pregnant with one of the slave's children, which led him to murder the slave and drove him to the point of insanity. When he allegedly learned that his other daughter was also pregnant by the slave's child, Payne murdered him and his entire family. He set his whole plantation on fire, which killed the rest of his slaves. In some versions of the story, Payne began worshipping the Devil and used the slaves for sacrificial rituals.

While the tale of Edward Payne is the most popular, there are a couple of other stories out there floating around about why the road is haunted. According to one of the legends, there was a young guy who got into a car crash near a chapel that once stood on the road where Edward Payne allegedly performed his Satan worship. The lore says that people watched and did nothing to help as the young man's car went up in flames and he burned to death. Some claim that you can see the rounded lights of the car the guy was driving when you travel Payne Road at night. The lights are thought to be his spirit.

The third story says that a family lived in the farmhouse during the 1800s. The husband decided that his children were the cause of him and his wife's arguments. He allegedly bound his wife to a chair, gagged her, and brought each of his children, one-by-one into the living room to tell their mother goodnight. He proceeded to take his children upstairs where he slit their throats. He decided to throw his infant daughter into the well, rather than slitting her throat. As he approached the well, his wife, who had managed to escape, attacked him and grabbed their daughter. Her husband caught her at the bridge, however, and decapitated her head with his knife. Then he threw the baby girl into the well before hanging himself from the bridge. According to local lore, you can see the ghost of the wife if you stop your car at the bridge and whistle "Dixie." The woman will allegedly appear, holding her head in her hands. There have also been reports of a baby crying from the well of the old farmhouse.

So, which of these stories is true? No one really knows for sure, but there's one thing that's certain. Many people report creepy occurrences on Payne Road. Like all creepy roads, there have been reports of people have car problems. Only drive this road in Rural Hall if you dare!

RANDOM FACTS

1. There have been numerous reports of UFO sightings in North Carolina. In fact, according to the National UFO Reporting Center, North Carolina ranks at No. 10 for the top states with the highest number of UFO reports. According to the center, North Carolina has had more than 2,800 sightings since the 1950s. It's safe to say you have a good chance of seeing a UFO during your next trip to the Tar Heel State!

2. North Carolina was once thought to be home to mermaids. While one might typically associate mermaids with the ocean, these mermaids were believed to live in the Cape Fear River near Greensboro, North Carolina. Legends of mermaids in this river date back to the 1700s. According to local lore, the mermaids were frequently spotted on a sandbar, which used to be known as Mermaid Point before it washed away after a dam flooded the area. Mermaids have not been spotted in the area since the flooding took place.

3. Like almost every state, North Carolina has a theater that's believed to be haunted. The Carolina Theatre in Greensboro is known for its

paranormal activity. The theater burned down back in 1981. A woman died in the fire. Today, many people claim that her spirit haunts the new Carolina Theatre, which was rebuilt where the old building once stood. People have claimed to see the woman's apparition and it's believed that her ghost is responsible for a number of odd incidences, such as unexplained noises, flickering lights, and opening and closing doors.

4. The oldest unsolved missing persons case in North Carolina involves two young brothers, six-year old Alan and eleven-year old Terry Westerfield, who disappeared in 1964. The day the boys went missing, their father dropped them off at the Broadway Movie Theatre in Fayetteville where they were meeting their mother. They were supposed to wait for her in the theater. When their mother arrived, however, they weren't there. Some of the movie theater workers had claimed to see them. Unfortunately, the critical 48-hour search period was affected by Hurricane Dora. The story made national headlines, with alleged sightings of the boys in states like Mississippi and Arizona. No real leads in the case were ever found, however. If the brothers are still alive, they would be in their 60s today.

5. Queens University in Charlotte, North Carolina is said to be one of the most haunted spots in the

state. Students have reported experiencing unexplained occurrences and paranormal activity for years. Some examples of this include doors that open and close on their own, unexplained knocking sounds, and flickering lights. Many people think the reason the university is haunted is because a former student committed suicide in the building. She allegedly killed herself when her parents learned that she was a lesbian.

6. The "Devil's Horse's Hoof Prints" are located near the town of Bath. They are small, saucer-shaped marks in the ground that are said to have been there since 1813. The indents measure 4-5" deep, with sloping sides that measure 6-10". According to local legend, a guy named Jesse Elliott and his friends had been racing their horses. Elliot allegedly told his horse to make him a winner or take him to Hell. The story says that the horse dug its hooved into the ground and threw Elliott against a tree, to his death. Believers of this legend think that the horse was the Devil's manifestation.

7. There have been numerous reports of Bigfoot sightings in North Carolina. With its mountains and forests, what better place for Sasquatch to hide out? Reports have been so plentiful in the state that there was even a research team in the Uwharrie National Forest searching for the

legendary creature. Researcher Lee Woods managed to capture a photo from the forest of a footprint that was 13″ long and 7″ wide. The footprint, which was casted, also had an unusual shape that appeared like it could only belonged to a Bigfoot. Woods also interviewed many people who claimed that they've seen the creature in the national forest. Others have reportedly heard strange, inhuman sounds that led them to hide in their tents. That being said, there are plenty of falsely reported sightings of Bigfoot as well. In 2019, there were reports of a "Bigfoot" with glowing red eyes, which turned out to be a statue. However, North Carolinians seem to believe in Bigfoot, for the most part. The WNC Bigfoot Festival is held in Marion, North Carolina each year in honor of the mythical creature.

8. The Bladenboro Poltergeist is one of North Carolina's creepiest legends. It all started out when Mrs. Charles Williamson, who was a housewife, had her dress catch on fire without any explainable cause or reason. Her husband and daughter were able to put out the flames, but they all questioned what could have caused it. Not too long after, a pair of shoes in Mrs. Williamson's closet also caught on fire—again for no reason. Over the course of the next four days,

the Williamsons' bed and curtains also caught on fire. There were also "spurts" of blue-flamed fire that would burn objects in the home. The fire was unable to be extinguished until the objects themselves were completely burned. The police were called, as well as electricians, but none of them could find any problem within the home that might have caused this to happen. After four days, the fires completely stopped. Fortunately, no one in the family was injured from the flames. With no explanation for the problem, people have wondered what caused the incident. A poltergeist is the most common theory, but the world will never know.

9. People have spotted a flickering light near Maco Station, which is a few miles west of Wilmington, NC. Even President Grover Cleveland claimed to see the lights while on tour in 1889. It's unknown what causes the lights, but plenty of people believe in the Maco Light legend. In 1867, a train wreck took place when the caboose got unattached from the train with sole occupant Joe Baldwin in it. A second passenger train was headed their way and Baldwin knew he had to do something to try to save everyone on board, so he stood on the back of the caboose with a lantern. The engineer of the second train saw Baldwin's warning signal, but he couldn't stop

the train in time. It hit into Baldwin's caboose, decapitating him. While many other lives were saved as a result of Baldwin's bravery, his own was lost. Since then, the flickering light has been seen near the site of the accident. Many believe that the Maco Light is Baldwin's spirit.

10. One of the worst train wrecks in history happened when a speeding train jumped the tracks and flew off the Bostian Bridge, which is located just west of Statesville. The tragic disaster, which happened on August 27th,1891, caused 23 fatalities. Rumor has it that ghostly apparitions can be seen from the bridge on the anniversary each year.

11. A house in the town of Tarboro is believed to be one of the most haunted houses in North Carolina due to a spine-chilling crime that happened there many years ago. The Mayo Family lived in the home. One night, Mr. Mayo fell into a rage that drove him to murder his family, including the family dog. Rumor has it that when Mr. Mayo finally came to, he was shocked by his own actions. Overcome with grief, he ended up hanging himself in the house. Today, it's said that the ghosts of the Mayo Family, along with the dog, welcome people into the house. If you go inside, the door will shut behind you. The family disappears. Many people

have claimed to see the apparition of a noose dangling above their heads as they enter the home.

12. Like other states, North Carolina is believed to have had its version of "fairies." The Moon-Eyed People are said to be a race of small men who lived in the southern Appalachian Mountains, according to the Cherokee. They were described as extremely pale, bearded men who lived in the underground caves. They were called the "Moon-Eyed People" because the sun bothered their eyes so much that they couldn't see in the daylight hours, leading them to be nocturnal. In some versions of the legends, the Cherokee went to war with the Moon-Eyed People, eventually driving them out of the Appalachian Mountains completely.

13. The Nunnehi are the Cherokee's other version of a "fairy." These fairy-like, little creatures were said to live under the ground in the southern Appalachian Mountains. The Nunnehi were tricksters, appearing before humans only when they wanted to and misleading humans by making their music sound close and then further away to confuse them about what direction they were hiding in. In one particular tale, the Nunnehi tricked Cherokee tribe members that they were Native American women from another

tribe. The Nunnehi weren't believed to be bad or evil creatures.

14. The Grove Park Inn is said to be one of the most haunted hotels in North Carolina. A number of guests have visited the hotel over years, but there's one who never left. During the 1920s, a woman who was wearing a pink gown fell from the 5th floor balcony and died. It's uncertain if her death was an accident or not. Some people believed that she was brokenhearted and intentionally threw herself off the balcony. Regardless of how she died, the Pink Lady is said to be seen walking the grounds and has also been reported in Room No. 545 where she plays pranks on guests staying in the room.

15. There's an old underpass known as Lydia's Bridge in Greensboro and its resident ghost is one of the most popular urban legends in the state. Drivers have claimed to see a young woman wearing a white dress on the side of the road trying to hitchhike on rainy nights. Those who have stopped for her have all reported having the same experience. The woman, who says her name is Lydia, gets into the back seat and says that she was just at a dance. She gives a nearby address and remains quiet for the rest of the car ride. However, the driver is always in for a big shock when he or she stops to let Lydia out

of the car and she's gone without a trace, disappearing into the night like any ghost would. She's said to be the spirit of a girl named Lydia who died in a car accident on the way home from her high school dance. According to the story, Lydia's heartbroken mother never left the house again after her daughter's death. She allegedly stayed in every night until her eventual death, hoping that her daughter would return back home.

16. The Great Dismal Swamp encompasses more than 100,000 acres along North Carolina's border and into Virginia. The swamp is a popular tourist attraction due to its natural beauty, but it's also believed to be haunted. People frequently report a strange feeling when they visit the Great Dismal Swamp. Some have also reported seeing strange and unexplained lights, mist-like apparitions, and eerie shadows. There have also been reports of unexplained noises.

17. Just about every state has a hospital that's said to be haunted and North Carolina is no exception. Davis Hospital in Statesville, North used to be a fully functional hospital. Now, the abandoned building is said to be one of the most haunted spots in the entire state. People who have visited the old hospital say that the building is always unnaturally cold, even on the hottest day of

summer. This is believed to be due to the spirits that still call the building their home. In addition to being unnaturally cold, the hospital is also said to leave visitors feeling unsettled. In the former pediatric ward, visitors have reported hearing babies crying and feeling an evil presence.

18. In 2007, 24-year-old Kyle Fleischmann went missing in Charlotte, North Carolina. He had been partying at an uptown nightclub. Fleischmann had first gone to a comedy show with his friends and then to the Buckhead Saloon. Kyle's friends left the bar sometime between 11 p.m. and 1 a.m. Surveillance footage showed a woman approaching Fleischmann right before the bar closed for the night. She and Kyle danced before she left with her boyfriend and two other guys. Footage showed Kyle leaving the bar alone. He hadn't taken his coat and debit card. He was last seen at a nearby Fuel Pizza. Then, Kyle tried to call his family and friends. It was believed that he was calling to find a ride. Kyle's father strongly believes that Kyle was killed and buried near a construction site. However, search teams never turned up anything in this area.

19. The Judaculla Rock in Jackson County may be North Carolina's most mysterious artifact. The soapstone is covered with hundreds of ancient markings. It's unknown what the carvings mean

or where they came from. Archaeologists who have studied the rock believe that the markings were carved 5,000 years ago and over the course of hundreds of years. However, there's an old Cherokee legend about the rock that says a giant might be responsible for the carvings. They believed the carvings to be the work of *Tsul`kälû´*, the name of a giant that allegedly lives in the area. The Cherokee believed this giant was over 7 feet tall, had 7 fingers and toes per hand and foot, claw-like fingernails, and was extremely hairy. Tsul`kälû´ also allegedly was in control of the wind, rain, thunder, and lightning and owned all of the game in the land, so the Cherokee had to gain his blessing if they wished to hunt. According to some variations of the Cherokee legend, the carvings on the Judaculla Rock were hunting laws that the giant wanted the tribe to obey. In another variation of the legend, the giant was angered that hunters had trespassed on his land and kicked the rock so hard that it left his footprint in it. Interestingly enough, there is a story in the lower righthand side of the Judaculla Rock that looks like a seven-toed foot.

20. Legend has it that there are skin-walkers in North Carolina. Although they are believed to be found throughout much of the state, the woods of Golden Valley are known to be a prime

location. Although skin-walkers are typically associated with Navajo culture, the Cherokee also believed in these medicine men or witches who could shift into an animal—typically a wolf or crow. Skin-walkers are said to be evil and often use their ability to shift to torment opposing tribes. They're also only believed to possess the ability to shift after killing a member of their own family.

Test Yourself – Questions

1. The Biltmore Estate is said to be home to the ghosts of George and Edith Vanderbilt, as well as:

   a. A headless Golden Retriever
   b. A headless orange cat
   c. A headless black cat

2. The Shadow of the Bear can be found every fall on which of North Carolina's mountains?

   a. Grandfather Mountain
   b. Mount Mitchell
   c. Whiteside Mountain

3. The ship that's today known as North Carolina's "ghost ship" is:

   a. The *USS* North Carolina
   b. Maynard's ship
   c. The *Carroll A. Deering*

4. The Devil's Tramping Ground is believed to be located near which of the following towns?

   a. Bennett, North Carolina
   b. Bladenboro, North Carolina
   c. Bath, North Carolina

5. Research teams have searched which of the following for Bigfoot?

   a. Uwharrie National Forest
   b. Pisgah National Forest
   c. Great Smoky Mountains National Park

Answers

1. b.

2. c.

3. c.

4. a.

5. a.

OTHER BOOKS IN THIS SERIES

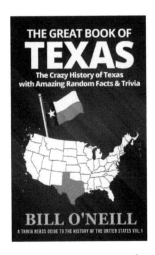

Are you looking to learn more about Texas? Sure, you've heard about the Alamo and JFK's assassination in history class, but there's so much about the Lone Star State that even natives don't know about. In this trivia book, you'll journey through Texas's history, pop culture, sports, folklore, and so much more!

In The Great Book of Texas, some of the things you will learn include:

Which Texas hero isn't even from Texas?

Why is Texas called the Lone Star State?

Which hotel in Austin is one of the most haunted hotels in the United States?

Where was Bonnie and Clyde's hideout located?

Which Tejano musician is buried in Corpus Christi?

What unsolved mysteries happened in the state?

Which Texas-born celebrity was voted "Most Handsome" in high school?

Which popular TV show star just opened a brewery in Austin?

You'll find out the answers to these questions and many other facts. Some of them will be fun, some of them will creepy, and some of them will be sad, but all of them will be fascinating! This book is jampacked with everything you could have ever wondered about Texas.

Whether you consider yourself a Texas pro or you know absolutely nothing about the state, you'll learn something new as you discover more about the state's past, present, and future. Find out about things that weren't mentioned in your history book. In fact, you might even be able to impress your history teacher with your newfound knowledge once you've finished reading! So, what are you waiting for? Dive in now to learn all there is to know about the Lone Star State!

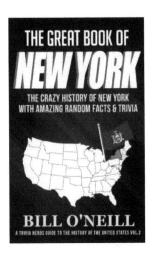

Want to learn more about New York? Sure, you've heard about the Statue of Liberty, but how much do you really know about the Empire State? Do you know why it's even called the Empire State? There's so much about New York that even state natives don't know. In this trivia book, you'll learn more about New York's history, pop culture, folklore, sports, and so much more!

In The Great Book of New York, you'll learn the answers to the following questions:

- Why is New York City called the Big Apple?
- What genre of music started out in New York City?
- Which late actress's life is celebrated at a festival held in her hometown every year?
- Which monster might be living in a lake in New York?

- Was there really a Staten Island bogeyman?
- Which movie is loosely based on New York in the 1800s?
- Which cult favorite cake recipe got its start in New York?
- Why do the New York Yankees have pinstripe uniforms?

These are just a few of the many facts you'll find in this book. Some of them will be fun, some of them will be sad, and some of them will be so chilling they'll give you goosebumps, but all of them will be fascinating! This book is full of everything you've ever wondered about New York.

It doesn't matter if you consider yourself a New York state expert or if you know nothing about the Empire State. You're bound to learn something new as you journey through each chapter. You'll be able to impress your friends on your next trivia night!

So, what are you waiting for? Dive in now so you can learn all there is to know about New York!

Are you interested in learning more about California? Sure, you've heard of Hollywood, but how much do you really know about the Golden State? Do you know how it got its nickname or what it was nicknamed first? There's so much to know about California that even people born in the state don't know it all. In this trivia book, you'll learn more about California's history, pop culture, folklore, sports, and so much more!

In The Great Book of California, you'll discover the answers to the following questions

- Why is California called the Golden State?
- What music genres started out in California?
- Which celebrity sex icon's death remains a mystery?
- Which serial killer once murdered in the state?
- Which childhood toy started out in California?

- Which famous fast-food chain opened its first location in the Golden State?
- Which famous athletes are from California?

These are just a few of the many facts you'll find in this book. Some of them will be entertaining, some of them will be tragic, and some of them may haunt you, but all of them will be interesting! This book is full of everything you've ever wondered about California and then some!

Whether you consider yourself a California state expert or you know nothing about the Golden State, you're bound to learn something new in each chapter. You'll be able to impress your college history professor or your friends during your next trivia night!

What are you waiting for? Get started to learn all there is to know about California!

MORE BOOKS BY BILL O'NEILL

I hope you enjoyed this book and learned something new. Please feel free to check out some of my previous books on Amazon.

IF YOU LIKED THIS BOOK, I WOULD REALLY APPRECIATE IF YOU COULD LEAVE A SHORT REVIEW ON AMAZON.